The Pop-Up Pastor

Set Your Priorities and Save Your Sanity

by Kevin McHann

Printed in the United States of America

First printing, 2018

ISBN 13-978-0-692-04757-6

For permission requests, speaking inquiries, and bulk order purchase options, email kevinmchann@gmail.com.

Dedicated to the beats of my heart:

Angie, my wife and friend, you are an amazing warrior

of love. You are my "forever and for always."

My two sons, Mason and Jordan, you fill me with joy.

Mallory, my wonderful daughter-in-love, you are the

missing link.

CONTENTS

FOREWORD
By Buddy Smith

Given the brokenness of the modern church, accepting the call of pastor can be daunting. This book addresses many of the trappings surrounding today's pastor and sounds urgent warnings that should become required reading for all preparing for pastoral ministry. Reading this book has been liberating. I will keep it in my library to recommend for pastors and lay leadership tasked with pastoral and staffing relations and oversight.

I was first introduced to Kevin McHann more than twenty years ago where his authentic witness for Jesus Christ was infectious and out of which flowed a passionate desire to serve God with all his heart. He was a gifted young songwriter and musician on fire to win the world to Christ.

Couple all that zeal to his youthful energies, and he was burning the candle at both ends in ministry at his local church and area evangelism. Now a much wiser and more seasoned pastor, Kevin issues a timely warning of the insanity, futility, and dangers for those he calls "Pop-Up" pastors or leaders who will do just about anything to please everyone around them.

The Great Commission will not happen if the work of the church is all done by the pastor and leadership.

Ministry in the church is intended not only for the highly gifted and trained specialists, but also for the entire body of Christ. When the pastor assumes the pop-up role, not only will there be burnout, but the laity is robbed of spiritual growth, and the mission of the church is short-circuited.

All these points and more are found in this book, which makes it an essential read, especially for pastors and leaders in the church or other ministry organizations.

—*Buddy Smith, senior vice president of American Family Association. Smith has been in ministry for more than forty-five years, twenty of those as a pastor.*

FOREWORD
By Jennifer Hand

When I was in my master's degree program in Christian counseling, the topic of burnout was often discussed. As professionals being trained to deal in soul care, our professors wanted to make sure we acknowledged the slippery slope that can lead to burnout in our own soul in this type of helping profession.

Although I have not studied pastoral ministries in seminary, I imagine a class on burnout and soul care for the pastor is not often included in class requirements.

I want to give *Pop-Up Pastor* to every person I know in pastoral ministry. This is a very practical toolbox full of steps to help anyone in ministry guard against the slippery slope that leads to exhaustion, burnout, disillusionment, and putting your family on the back burner.

I have had the blessing of knowing Pastor Kevin for several years and was so blessed to follow his journey in the chapters of this book. His honesty and transparency will help pastors (or anyone in ministry), seasoned and brand new, examine their own hearts and ministry philosophies. The themes in these chapters will lead you to purify ministry motives, release expectations, and minister out of stronger emotional health.

As a counselor, I have seen the effects burnout and exhaustion can have on pastors, missionaries, and other ministers. It is my belief that this book will be an amazing resource to help prevent ministers from reaching the point where they are unable to effectively minister.

I love how the pages of this book gently encourage us in our ministry callings to dream big but to be able to watch God do bigger things than we can ask or imagine, not because we "pop up" to fulfill every ministry need but because we partner with others, recognize our limitations, and examine our motivations.

The gentle, humble, and transparent approach of this book will be an inviting voice of wisdom to any pastor in your life. As someone in full-time ministry myself, each chapter and page caused me to do my own self-examination. I found freedom and conviction as I read, and I believe you will also.

If you are currently in ministry, or praying about pursuing your calling, I encourage you to read this book with an open heart and be prepared to use the tools to keep you in the ministry long term.

All of us know someone who needs the tools in this practical toolbox.

—*Jennifer Hand, Executive Director of Coming Alive Ministries and author of* Confessions of a Coffee Cup

Collector, 31 Days to Coming Alive, 25 Days to Coming
Alive at Christmas, and Coming Alive at the Cross

CHAPTER ONE

The Pop-Up Pastor

I f you've ever found yourself struggling to be everywhere, for everything, and for everyone every time, or if you're someone who is entering into ministry and feel what you are doing isn't enough, this book is for you. If you are embarking upon a leadership opportunity, this could be a helpful word that can save you some heartache before you find yourself asking where you went wrong. Maybe, just maybe, I could take a few pages to encourage the burdened heart and possibly warn those of you in ministry of the dangers of trying to be everywhere, for everything, and for everyone every time, also known as "The Pop-Up Pastor!"

Within every person, there is an innate yearning to be liked by others and please everyone you possibly can. First, there's nothing wrong with that in and of itself. God designed us to have and build relationships. He also created us and encourages us to live in peace with all men *(Romans 12:18)*.

However, don't err on the first part of that scripture. "If it is possible, as far as it depends on you…" "If" is the word that carries a lot of question and doubt. "If" it is possible. There seems to be some question whether it's possible to please everyone. Let's go ahead and set the record straight. We will never please everyone. Jesus Himself never pleased everyone. Too many doubted, too many hated who He claimed to be, and too many just didn't like what He said. So guess what? Neither will you! I use the term "Pop-Up Pastor" to describe a minister or leader who will do just about anything to basically please everyone around them. When you think about it, ministry should be joyful, passionate, and sincere—not creating the kind of stress that causes families to split, causes children to detach themselves from the family, and induces avoidable pressures and obligations. As a pastor or leader, you will love what you do. You will have self-motivation. You will have drive and passion with sincerity for a lost and dying world. The problem is when you try to be more than what you are designed to be. Ordained structure outlined in scripture is God's design for those serving others. It is this structure that must be followed and practiced. Deviating from this structure is the first step in failure. Deviating from this structure will lead you straight through the door to be the next Pop-Up Pastor.

As a small boy, I always enjoyed having someone read to me. But what was even better was when they would read what is known as a pop-up book. I could see the book come to life by the projectile thrust of the surprise pop-up book. I was amazed at how much was compressed into such a small book. I marveled at every turned page when a new character or scene would magically explode into a 3-D scene. Many years later, a thought came to mind that led me to think of that pop-up book. I imagined what life would be like if we had the possibility of living with pop-up capabilities.

What if, when you had some amazing news, all of your close family and friends could instantaneously pop up to join you in the celebration. What if, when your day has been less than productive, your mom could just pop up and give you a warm hug, which by the way, makes everything better. What if during a time of need, someone could pop up and be there for you. It might sound a lot like a genie in a bottle. You rub the bottle, summoning a genie in order to acquire your three wishes. If only life were that simple, that quick, and that accessible.

You see, the principle of the pop-up book became an important life lesson for me several years ago, revealing a vicious cycle, much like an addiction. I had become a prisoner of my own device of repeating the same embarrassing and defeating cycle of poor planning and misplaced priorities. It didn't take long for me to realize I wasn't the only one who had succumbed to this self-affliction.

Let's go back to my childhood for a moment. As a young boy, I was raised in a Christian family. I was taken to church every time the doors were open, whether I wanted to go or not. Being in and around the church world, I saw and heard a lot of things—some amazing and some not so much. I learned who the pastor was and what he did. And through the years, I was taught to have respect for the pastor and honor his calling. I continue that respect and honor to this day.

However, there was a point and time in which I placed pastors well above a healthy perspective. The way I once perceived the pastor and the church is quite humorous now. In my mind, I placed God at the top, followed by the pastor. He was someone who did no wrong, who was perfect, and who had EVERYTHING together. Wow, was I wrong! Wait! I'm not throwing the pastor under the bus.

I'm recognizing that no man is perfect. No, I haven't lost respect and reverence for the pastor—nor should you. It was just that I had extolled him in such a way that I never questioned his words nor his actions. I elevated him higher than I should have. I deemed him to be holier than thou. It wasn't that he felt this way, but it was my perception. For all I knew, the pastor lived at the church. And I believed that whatever he said, God said, and that was all that was to be said!

I never thought he was God, but it did seem that he at least had some special hotline connection with Him. It appeared that he knew every time someone had a need. By some chance, he would just show up. Somehow, he would just magically appear at every function, dinner, fundraiser, wedding, funeral, hospital room, baseball game, garage sale, and anything else the congregation expected. He was like Superman! I could picture him getting a call, running into his office, and three seconds later coming back out dressed in a white-winged spandex suit ready to fly off to the next assignment. He WAS Superman in my book.

It was years later that I came to realize he was just like me. He sweated, he got hungry, he put on pants like I did, he went to the grocery store like I did, and he had struggles like I did. One of those struggles was he wanted to be liked by everyone. He did his best to do the right thing. He went out of his way to be something or someone for another. He sacrificed many of his own desires for the sake of the flock. It all seemed awesome that someone would do this for others. The only challenge was, "How could he be everywhere, for everything, and for everyone all the time?" Ding, ding, ding! Not possible! He was attempting to be at every function, party, hospital visit, nursing home, and celebration. The question was, "How could he just pop up everywhere?"

That is a good question. The truth of the matter is, he couldn't. How could anyone possibly be at everyone's events? What about his own family? How could he be everywhere for everyone else and his own family as well? Now please don't misunderstand me. Leading, shepherding, and caring for the flock IS a pastor's heart, vision, and job. Being a pastor myself, I know that. But I also realize your family is your ministry.

The sobering fact is that we as pastors can't handle it all by ourselves, no matter the size of the heart for the people.

Another truth of leadership is that the larger the flock, the more responsibility that is required. And the larger the flock is, the more delegation that is required, which leads to more pastoring hearts who are needed to facilitate the care for each person. There's one indisputable fact regarding a true pastor's heart. His heart aches and yearns for the flock to be reached, saved, and nurtured. The sobering fact is that we as pastors can't handle it all by ourselves, no matter the size of the heart for the people.

Several years ago, sitting in a staff meeting, we were going over prayer requests from individuals of our local congregation. This meeting was no different from any other meetings we had been accustomed too. However, as we began reading the requests from the people of the congregation, an overwhelming panic came over me. Some were asking prayer for lost loved ones, family members fighting terminal illnesses, financial burdens, and so much more. The more I read, the heavier my heart became. It was in that moment the realization of being powerless flooded my mind. It was a moment I will never forget. My heart felt the pain of those in suffering, those in pain, those in grief. To be honest, I wanted to walk out of that meeting and run for the hills or take wings of a bird and fly away from it all. How could we as individuals bear so much need? I felt powerless because I wanted to be everywhere, every time, for everybody, yet I couldn't. My heart felt the anguish of those who were at that very moment facing crisis. How could I be there for them?

Well, the answer came quickly as I was reminded that God is God and I am not! I couldn't be there for each person. But I knew the Father could. He hears our prayers and He loves us more than we can comprehend. I simply wanted to be there for everyone and be what others needed. To be completely honest, I still struggle with it. But then again, that's why we need each other. We are a body working together. Yet, I've tried to do it on my own many times since. Note to self: It ain't working!

As I continued to mature and learn, I began to notice a pattern that would affect not only me but others in the future. This pattern was honorable but not necessarily healthy. I watched many pastors succumb to this pattern that I call, Paul-ism, or the Pop-Up Pastor.

Who is the Pop-Up Pastor? Well, it derives its definition from yours truly! This perspective is rooted in 1 Corinthians 9:22, the passage where the apostle Paul said he would become all things to all people in order to win some. Yes, he was going to do what he could, sacrifice his own desires and wants, and be what God wanted of him. The difference is when you become a victim of your own busyness and not an effective minister of Christ. Paul's efforts were not about busyness but about being effective. His mindset was on being an effective witness by becoming the very thing others needed. He wasn't trying to reach one hundred percent of everyone everywhere, but instead he made sure he gave his one hundred percent to everyone he met everywhere. Paul was in a season of his life when he could devote his time to the Lord.

The dynamics change when we have spouses and children, and these dynamics are affected by attempting to be the great Pop-Up person all rolled in one. When you try to be everywhere, for everyone, every time, you will find yourself trapped in a vicious cycle that is difficult to break. A cycle that is never satisfied. A cycle, which you, by habitual ignorance, fall prey to over and over again. This miscalculated cycle threatens the very core of relationships. There have been numerous pastors who have either lost their families or at least weakened the fabric of their relationships by trying to accomplish impossible means by themselves.

Placing others over your own family and their needs is not only costly, but it's also not scriptural.

Ministers, who have walked into this plight of leadership, fail because they have sacrificed families just to accommodate others. They had a blurred vision of success—not that serving others is the culprit. No, service is the crux of the gospel. Scripture instructs us to put the needs of others over our own, as found in Philippians 2:3. Placing others over your own family and their needs is not only costly, but it's also not scriptural. The command of putting "others" first is right. Just don't forget that your family is "others" too.

Taking a moment to review where relationships first began, you must go back to the book of Genesis. God created man and woman. He told them to multiply. He ordained the family and placed the man as the priest of that family God blessed and entrusted him with. Whenever someone deviates from that, ordination will suffer. Remember, it's not just one who suffers but the whole. You can make it your goal to meet everyone's events and occasions, but it will be at the price of your own family and that price is the costliest of all debts. God initiated families. He planned and purposed men to be the priests of their homes. Being the priest of your own home means your first responsibility of ministry IS your very own family. Your mission is to pour what you have into the lives of your children. In scripture, we read that God instructed fathers as they go, they are to teach their children—when they rise, lie down, during their going and their coming. Ministry to your family never ends. It is an ongoing nurturing and privilege. It is a priority and necessity for our own households to be households of faith! It's not enough to have head knowledge of Jesus or an association with Jesus, but that each one *knows* their relationship with Jesus.

Secondly, it says, "as far as it depends on you." You have to be responsible for yourself and your own actions. You cannot control others and how or what they think. I believe one of the most difficult lessons for ministers to learn is the fact that we are not God! No, no one would intentionally say this, but by our actions we non-verbally express this message. It's possible that our desires to accomplish tasks or situations can be so strong that our own lusts for success drive us to a place that only God can be. I know this sounds harsh and may actually hit us between the eyes, but it's one truth that we'd better learn early. Attempting to be everywhere, for everybody, every time is something many struggle with and fail miserably at it. Does God want us to work hard to be everything for everybody all the time?

Third, we were never meant to accomplish God's design and plans alone. Let me say that again. Stop trying to accomplish ministry alone. Jesus didn't! Matthew 10:2 gives the names of the ones whom He would use to change the world. Through all of the gospels, scriptures tell us Jesus took twelve broken, misguided, and sinful men and poured into their lives, commanding them to change the world. So if Jesus set that example of multiplication, then so should we. The church that Jesus set up was never set up in order for one person to be the star of the show. In fact, it's just the opposite. He designed the church to be communal—a body that would move together. He positioned twelve men who would have the same vision, passion, and goals in order to change the world for the Kingdom.

Unfortunately, not everyone adopts the blueprints for ministry Jesus designed. 1 Corinthians 1:13-14 gives the account where, you got it, believers were arguing over who was more important.

> "Is Christ divided? Was Paul crucified for you? Or were ye baptized in the name of Paul? I thank God that I baptized none of you, but Crispus and Gaius." (*1 Corinthians 1:13-14*)

When I read this, I can't help but picture Paul shaking his head in disbelief that believers would be so blinded by self-righteousness, shaking his head over the fact that people were willing to split the unity in Christ over who was following which man of God instead of following Christ himself.

It all comes down to who and what this "life change" is all about. It's all about Christ! We are His disciples, we are His feet, His hands, His voice, and His heart to those who are lost and hurting. If we get caught up in ourselves, we will miss the greatest opportunities known to man: the salvation of many! Throughout these pages you will hear time and time again that our best attempt at being everywhere, for everything, and for everyone every time is futile.

If we fly solo, we will experience the frustrations and disappointments of that attempt. I know there are some who feel the need to be all to everyone. I did too. Those feelings can be driven by self-motivation or by example from others. It is imperative we always remember there is a design and purpose for God's plan and we are divinely called to help facilitate that purpose and plan.

He called and chose those who were pliable and hungry for change.

You see, Jesus surrounded Himself with twelve weather-worn, abrasive, unlearned, and stubborn men in order to teach them about His purpose, His calling, and His plan. He poised them to be coworkers in the kingdom, to spread the gospel. He chose men who would be free from preconceived ideas of who He was. He called and chose those who were pliable and hungry for change. Jesus met them at their point of decision. After spending some time with Jesus, they realized His mission was larger than themselves. Yet, we, by ourselves, embark upon the futile attempt, over and over again, to accomplish the vision and dreams God has placed in us. Yes, the struggle is real and we have to find that balance in order to be effective and not just busy. This is the reason for this book.

The reason I feel I am credible to write on this subject is that I was one of those pastors who not only fell into this trap but failed several times. Even though I've changed my perception of what ministry is over the past several years, I still find the struggle to be real. Why? It's the same reason any passionate pastor does it: I love what I do and love being with people. I love helping people. But what good have I done or what accolades have I deserved if I only met the needs of others and not my family the Father has so graciously poured into my life? What example have I left for others to follow if I put family second? What good have I done if I travel across the seas to help others but cannot step into the life of my own son? What good have I done if my name is known throughout the world yet unknown to my own family? What have I done if I've shaken hands with thousands of people but lost the grip of unity with my own children?

The power of influence on your own family is powerful. You have the awesome opportunity to pour into each member of your household. You have what no one else has and that is to live out your faith in front of your family. Your influence on your sons and daughters is priceless; your influence on your spouse is immeasurable. If you are going to fail at something, fail at being the worst parent ever!

CHAPTER TWO

Make Every Moment Matter

"Daddy, Daddy, do you have to leave again?" My four-year-old son whimpered. Those words stunned me as if I had just run into a door face first. What an eye opener! I had been traveling for a couple of years ministering in kids' crusades with a typical annual travel of one hundred and fifty days. I had been so busy trying to be everywhere for everybody else that I nearly missed precious moments with my own sons. I wanted to be successful. I felt I needed to be on the move. I felt if I didn't stay on the go, then the business of ministry would fail. My passion drove me, and I never touched the brakes to slow down.

If you have experienced this before, let me ask you to stop for a moment and define the passion driving you. What was the passion about? Who would the success of this passion satisfy? When you stop to evaluate your own life, I believe you will discover some truths. Ask yourself this question. Is this passion God-given or self-initiated? If you have a passion from God, it will burn in you. Yes, you will be consumed with passion and a drive to do all you are able to do. However, without a plan and strategy, you will be overrun by it. The one passion God gives all of us is this: to love the Lord with all your heart, soul, mind, and strength. Then it's followed by loving our neighbors as ourselves *(Mark 12:30-31)*. These two commands from scripture are important. When you stop to think about it, every program or event is designed and/or facilitated by us. It's what we do to reach others. But have we missed the closest harvest field in our reach, the family? Yes, all of the programs, events, and outreaches are vital in reaching others. I'm just stating that if we do not delegate and balance our time, plan, and strategize, then our time will be dictated by the demands we ourselves have created.

Now, back to my story of my son. How could I have been so blind? How could I have been so self-indulged that I couldn't see the need of my own son for his father? Why had I made him of less value than another child? Not intentionally, but by my absence. My unrestrained drive for success took me further than I needed to be. My son needed me, his daddy, to stop and give him the attention he desperately needed. I had to intentionally make time for him.

There was a song written in 1974 by Harry Chapin called *Cats in the Cradle*. If there is ever a song that can hit a dad between the eyes of his heart, it would most definitely be this one. This song is a story of a dad who had a son but was so busy in life that he missed out spending time with him. When the young boy got older he wanted to be just like his dad. Dad always promised some day they would get together, but it never happened. Years pass, and the young man is now in college and living his life on his own. Finally, the song reveals later years when the dad has retired. He calls his son asking for a visit, but the grown son doesn't have the time to come home, and the old man realizes his son is just like him. Allow me to share the lyrics with you.

My child arrived just the other day
He came to the world in the usual way
But there were planes to catch, and bills to pay
He learned to walk while I was away

And he was talking 'fore I knew it, and as he grew

He'd say, I'm gonna be like you, Dad

You know I'm gonna be like you

And the cat's in the cradle and the silver spoon

Little boy blue and the man in the moon

When you coming home, Dad?

I don't know when

But we'll get together then

You know we'll have a good time then

My son turned ten just the other day

He said, thanks for the ball, Dad, come on let's play

Can you teach me to throw, I said, not today

I got a lot to do, he said, that's okay

And he walked away, but his smile never dimmed

Said, I'm gonna be like him, yeah

You know I'm gonna be like him

And the cat's in the cradle and the silver spoon

Little boy blue and the man in the moon

When you coming home, Dad?

I don't know when

But we'll get together then

You know we'll have a good time then

Well, he came from college just the other day

So much like a man I just had to say

Son, I'm proud of you

Can you sit for a while?

He shook his head, and he said with a smile

What I'd really like, Dad, is to borrow the car keys

See you later

Can I have them please?

And the cat's in the cradle and the silver spoon

Little boy blue and the man in the moon

When you coming home, Dad?

I don't know when

But we'll get together then

You know we'll have a good time then

I've long since retired and my son's moved away

I called him up just the other day

I said, I'd like to see you if you don't mind

He said, I'd love to, Dad, if I could find the time

You see, my new job's a hassle, and the kid's got the flu

But it's sure nice talking to you, Dad

It's been sure nice talking to you

And as I hung up the phone, it occurred to me

He'd grown up just like me

My boy was just like me

And the cat's in the cradle and the silver spoon

Little boy blue and the man in the moon

When you coming home, Dad?

I don't know when

But we'll get together then

You know we'll have a good time then

Writer/s: HARRY F. CHAPIN, SANDY CHAPIN

Publisher: Warner/Chappell Music, Inc.

Repeatedly, people scurry from here to there, searching for the next "big" thing when the "best" things are right under their care. My own father recognized this early on and made necessary changes in order to redeem the time with his family. When I was young, my father's occupation required him to travel away from home. His schedule was very demanding. I recall him coming home on Friday evenings, going to eat as family, and hanging out at home. Then early every Saturday morning, he would take me to the local café that was on Main Street in Starkville, Mississippi. He made me feel like I was as important as any other man in the café. We had the same breakfast, which was two eggs, over easy, with biscuits and bacon. I tried my best to sit like he did, eat like he did, and act like he did. It was a great time.

I also recall Dad taking my brother and me horseback riding on those late Saturday mornings. From time to time, we would load up with a snack and go fishing at our favorite pond, which belonged to family members. Saturday evenings we would watch TV together as a family or play games. One of my favorite games, hide and seek, was actually played with our fox terrier named Skeeter. My brother and I would run and hide while Dad covered Skeeter's eyes. Then, after counting to ten, Dad would let Skeeter come find us. When he did, he would try his best to nip our toes. For some reason, he just loved getting my brother's toes more than mine. The highlight of the weekend was when we all got dressed, loaded in the car, and made our way to church as a family. Once church was over, we gave our hugs, kisses, and the words, "Daddy, do you have to go?" On Monday, he would have to travel back to his job site.

As a few years passed, I recall the day he was supposed to go back to work. It was a Sunday afternoon. We were outside playing together when his coworkers drove up to our house to pick up my dad. When I saw the car that would take my dad away, I became heartbroken. I said something that day that I really didn't mean nor would I ever say intentionally. I asked him, "Do you have to go?" He assured me he did.

At that moment at the top of my lungs I screamed, "Then leave and don't ever come back!" That day, my dad—in one of the most courageous and boldest acts I will ever know—turned in his notice. He stayed that evening and explained why he had to go. But just in a short time, he came home to be with his family.

Dad, thank you so much for that life lesson and the unconditional love you showed me. I love and miss you!

Instead of attempting to be everywhere, for everything, and for everyone every time, he changed the course of our family. For that I am forever grateful. You see, he not only changed the course for us, but for those God has blessed me with.

Think about time for a moment. That moment is gone. You see, time is more valuable than any other commodity. Once you use it, you never get it back. Once a moment passes, it is lost in the gulf of history. Each moment matters. Each minute matters. So, learning what's important and prioritizing those moments are crucial. If there is one regret people have more often than any other, it is the regret of how they spent their time. Time management is the sanity among the screams of responsibilities. In the book of James, he reminds us with

If there is one regret people have more often than any other, it is the regret of how they spent their time.

28

all soberness that our lives are only for a moment compared to eternity.

"Why, you do not even know what will happen tomorrow. What is your life? You are a mist that appears only for a little while and then vanishes." (*James 4:14*)

This passage unquestionably and soberly reveals the quantity of time we so easily squander. Without evaluating how you spend your time, you'll never value the time you do have to spend. The very fact that we use the word "spend" to describe our usage of time implies time is costly. Time costs. Giving of yourself to ministry will take time. Taking time out of your day to manage your time will actually yield more time for other things. So, protect your time.

Prioritizing is the wall of protection that will keep you from squandering this precious gift.

Earth is full of amazing animals. All are either prey or predator. One of the most amazing predators is the lion which can be found in the Serengeti. Interesting enough, lions are very strategic hunters. One of their favorite meals is the wildebeest. As the wildebeests begin their arduous migration, the impregnated genus of antelopes brings new life by giving birth to their offspring. Thousands of newborn calves touch the Earth for the first time with wobbly legs and a keen sense of dependency upon their mothers. As beautiful as this may be, there remains a harsh reality. As these newborn calves are learning to walk and run, they face a grave danger of being targeted as a meal. The hard truth is that many of these young calves fall prey to the king of the Serengeti. The lions intentionally create chaos in order to break up the herd so the young wildebeests are left abandoned. The only saving grace for these juvenile calves is when the mothers and other members of the herd surround them to create a wall of protection.

I use this analogy to express the importance of protecting your time. You must protect your time as the most precious commodity you have—for it is. Predators of your time such as busyness, demands, and the lack of delegating, to name a few, lie in wait for the first sign of abandonment by the lack of prioritizing. Prioritizing is the wall of protection that will keep you from squandering this precious gift called time.

You see, ministry has never been, nor will it ever be, the problem. However, the lack of prioritizing will be. A pastor friend once told me as I was navigating through the venues of ministry, "You won't have to be concerned about *will* there be ministry to be involved with, but you will have to choose *which* ministry to be involved with."

All ministry efforts are important. All ministry is beneficial. All ministries are priority. However, you cannot accomplish "all" ministries alone. If you could do it all then you would have to omit Ephesians 4:11-12 from scripture:

"And He gave some, apostles; and some, prophets; and some, evangelists; and some, pastors and teachers; For the perfecting of the saints, for the work of the ministry, for the edifying of the body of Christ."

God gave different people different passions to accomplish different objectives for the purpose of building His kingdom. God never designed it for us to do it all ourselves, nor do it all alone. He made us so we would need each other. He made us to be better together. Remember, in Genesis, God said that it was not good that man be alone? He designed for the first man, Adam, to have a helpmate. This woman was made to accompany Adam and absorb some of the responsibility in life.

Please don't misinterpret the idea here. There are many pastors, leaders, and workers who have tremendous amounts of pressure from their ministry responsibilities and do the best they can. However, just imagine how many of them could enjoy the benefits of this life with less stress, fewer physical problems brought on by stress, and less burnout if they would delegate and prioritize? When we prioritize our tasks our time, and our lives, we will experience great peace. Unless we strategically plan and prioritize for the dream, we will never accomplish that dream to its full potential.

CHAPTER THREE

Influence and Delegate

I love old Westerns—well, just about any Western movie, old or new. I love the ones where a gang of outlaws comes riding into town, striking fear into the people. The streets are cleared as the citizens run and hide. At that moment, the rising hope is found in the newly appointed sheriff and he's going to bring the strong arm of law and justice. But there were times when the sheriff would be outnumbered, and the people doubted his ability to preserve their town and restore their hope. In that pivotal moment in time, there was one thing the sheriff would do when he realized he was outnumbered. He would select brave and valiant men he could deputize. These men formed what was called a posse. He would then take that posse and accomplish the insurmountable task of bringing those vile gangsters to justice one by one.

It's the same principle in ministry. You as a pastor, leader, and shepherd cannot manage a dream alone, much less all the demands that naturally come with the position. You have to deputize men of integrity to help round up all those loose bandits who will rob you of your time and effectiveness.

In the early '50s, *The Lone Ranger* series was introduced. The Lone Ranger was a masked former Texas Ranger who fought outlaws in the West. The TV series lasted for several years and has since been rerun even to this day. In 2013, he was reintroduced in the movie called *The Lone Ranger*, starring Johnny Depp and Armie Hammer. The Lone Ranger was a solo act until he met a Native American who would become his best friend and partner in pursuing justice. His name was Tonto. He was the support system and the go-to guy for the Lone Ranger.

One lesson learned very early is that no one can do what they are to do by themselves. We all need those around us to help keep our sanity and focus. But, if you are pulling the Lone Ranger card, then guaranteed, you will not be effective. You must acquire some Tontos who will buy into the vision, catch the dream, and run with power.

You know, there is a principle that applies here, and that is "refusing to expand is refusing to grow." This is where the problem lies. When the dream or vision is bigger than your abilities, you must delegate. Instead of attempting to be everywhere and everything for everybody, you do what no one else can do and bring others along to do what they can do. Bring on the deputies!

When I began in ministry, I knew very little about the ins and outs of being part of a church staff. I knew very little about the demands and expectations of ministry. I knew very little of what it would mean to go all out in my dreams and goals. I really had no idea how new and green I really was. All I knew was I

Refusing to expand is refusing to grow.

had a deep desire to do something great for God. So, when the opportunity came to be in full-time ministry at a church, I accepted the position. Little did I know just how this opportunity would bring liberation of ministry in my life. I never knew the magnitude of how someone could be empowered to do ministry. The senior pastor extended his hands of blessings and permission to chase after my heart's desires. He empowered me by affirming my value, first as a Christian, second as a children's minister, and third as one who had a vision to move forward doing what I dreamt of doing. Wow! I couldn't believe my ears. He spoke life to my dreams and goals!

Let me use an analogy from *The Wizard of Oz*. Before this pastor empowered me, I felt as if I had been operating in a black-and-white world, much like Dorothy's life prior to the tornado. Then, when he affirmed my calling, it felt as if that pivotal door was opened and I stepped into the most beautiful colors of a new world. I was able to move forward with great anticipation and passion. It was an awesome time in ministry and I can't thank him enough for the opportunity to grow in an incredible journey. It was an amazing time of increase. In order for that increase to happen, there had to be an expansion—an expansion of learning, an expansion full of trials, and an expansion of my own thinking. I had to learn! I learned what not to do when I tried accomplishing dreams and goals by myself. I had to learn to expand. I had to learn to delegate. I had to learn to let others inside my world, my goals, my dreams, and my thoughts. I had to allow my wineskin to be stretched in order to hold more. Once my thinking changed, so did my dreams and goals. They became bigger!

The prayer of Jabez is an awesome prayer, but if you are praying for more increase but aren't willing to expand, it will never happen *(1 Chronicles 4:10)*. It would be as futile as trying to grasp a puddle of water in your hand and expecting it to remain. It won't work!

As mentioned before, the scriptures tell us everything has been written so we will not make the same mistakes, falling in the same traps and suffering the same pains many did so long ago. The Bible is full of people who made some mistakes, but not all were intentional failures. Not all failures were planned. Some were made for the same reason we do things—passion and responsibility.

Let me explain by using the story of Moses. He was judge and leader of the children of Israel. He was their go-to leader. He was "that guy" whom everyone trusted as their judge. I can just imagine Moses sitting in his designated seat with a line of people, similar to the lines you might see at an amusement park, waiting to be heard. Not every case was easy. Not every case was cut and dry. Not every case was quick. It may have been similar to standing in line at the DMV. Yet through it all, I'm sure Moses did his best at being everything for everybody every time. Come to think of it, ol' Moses could possibly have been the first Pop-Up Pastor. Can you imagine Moses having to be everywhere, every time, for everybody? Well, that's pretty much what he attempted to do. He was much like many pastors who feel obligated to be the one who has to be every place, for every person, every time they needed him.

Who was this Moses? He was just a Hebrew raised in the courts and home of the Pharaoh himself. He was a leader who had trouble speaking because of a speech impediment. He was just a guy who was leading a few million people who all had issues, problems, and dilemmas. Maybe in Moses's mind, he felt he WAS the only one qualified to judge, which created a multitude of problems.

The Bible says after a period of time, Moses's father-in-law, Jethro, came for a visit and witnessed the futility of this unruly system. Jethro witnessed firsthand what Moses was attempting to do, which was hear and judge all the issues of the children of Israel. The problem was not that Moses was hearing cases that were small and trivial or of great importance. The problem was that Moses was attempting to address each and every one of the cases. He was doing his best to be everything for everybody, every time. He couldn't possibly hear every case. Can you imagine hundreds or possibly thousands of people lined up just to get a fair judgment from Moses? Impossible! Jethro recognized and identified the commendable, yet unattainable, feat of hearing and resolving every case. For Moses it would only lead to frustration and pressure.

Jethro advised Moses, "Moses, what you desire is admirable, but your system is broken!" Jethro knew even though Moses had the goods as a great leader, he wouldn't or couldn't accomplish the task by himself.

Did Moses feel the need to be everything to everybody all the time? Sounds like it! Whether intentional or unintentional, he was building for himself a structure that would fall to ruin. Jethro's instruction was very timely. Exodus 18:13-26 states that he instructed Moses to appoint leaders, and Moses did everything he advised him to do. The most important part of this lesson is, Moses followed instruction. Please hear what the scripture says. When the dream, vision, or task becomes larger than your ability to sufficiently tend the demands, then we should learn to delegate.

Remember, without expanding you will remain the same. Oh, and by the way, delegating isn't weakness. It's wisdom. Without delegation, you can only climb so high. Some people are the hands-on type, and that's OK to a certain extent. But if you are to grow, you must take your hands off and allow the hands of someone else to increase what you have already begun. You can only do so much. If you can't delegate, then maybe you should look inside to discover why. Is it that you too feel you are the only one who can adequately and proficiently accomplish a task?

Hopefully what you do isn't for selfish ambition. I realize there are some who feel the need to do it all themselves. Perhaps some desire the recognition of completing an incredible task solo. Doing ministry should never be self-seeking or self-edifying. When we make ministry about ourselves, it typically means we crown ourselves with the right to boast in the fact we are the only ones suffering, the only ones giving it all in sacrifice, and the only ones who can accomplish the task. Don't seek the honor; it belongs to God! Don't seek the glory; it's God's too! And most of all, don't try to be God. You're not!

Moses learned his lesson. He realized the dream of taking millions of people to the Promised Land was much larger than he ever imagined. I, for one, can easily find myself struggling to accomplish all that needs to be done due to the lack of delegating. There's an old saying—actually a question—about how to accomplish great things. That question is, "How do you eat an elephant? One piece at a time."

When you first hear the question, your mind automatically calculates the size of the elephant, realizing you can't—not at one sitting. So, how do you accomplish big dreams? One step at a time, one delegated piece at a time. Dreams, visions, and goals never end. Neither does delegation. But if a leader doesn't exemplify a balanced life, then those being mentored will be affected.

As I mentioned previously, a pastor's example can sabotage a younger minister's life when he's attempting to be everywhere, for everything, and for everyone every time. Not only does this absurdity set up failure for the younger pastor, which is a lot to assume, but it is also setting up a congregation for unrealistic expectations. How? If a senior pastor were to get a call about a member in the hospital and he visits the patient, then the next member or attendee will expect the same. There is nothing wrong with being there for them. The problem I'm speaking of is being expected to be at every event for every person. Great idea, but there's only one of you. You can guarantee each person will expect the same attention you are showing others before them. You do realize you can't fulfill that expectation, right? This is another setup for hurt and disappointment. The time you aren't able to be there for each one, well, there's rarely a full recovery because people assume you care for others more than you do them. There has to be healthy and realistic expectations from the congregation. When the congregation is unrealistic in their expectations, they literally absorb all of your time no matter the sacrifice or cost upon you or your family. All the more reason for delegation.

Pastors have the ability to create a culture where people will either follow them or follow God. Pastors, either by their intentional or unintentional principles, can lead people to be dependent on them and their lead rather than leading others to move forward in following God. Most pastors would never intentionally plan to draw people to themselves. But having success in ministry tempts pastors to take credit for what God is doing. Bad decision! When we celebrate success, we must be careful to give God *all* of the glory and praise, for it is He who has allowed us to participate in His work. Pastors hold sacred credibility with people, but when it is abused, it can lead many to false hope and wounding disappointment.

History is filled with world leaders, spiritual powerhouses, athletic phenoms, military greats, and intellectual geniuses who have led people to salvation or an early grave, all because of influence. When you stop and think about it, we are all influenced by someone at some point in our lives. Someone's actions, decisions, and reactions can easily be understood when you take a look at who their influences in life have been, especially as a young child. Influence is powerful. Most movie stars, musicians, or political leaders will tell you someone who impacted their lives by something that they did or said. Influence is linked to those who have preceded us.

Professional athletes carry more influence than they readily admit. They can become idolized by young men and women who have aspirations to become great athletes like them. Some athletes understand the mantle of greatness. They wear it with humility and understanding that they are no different than anyone else but skilled in doing what they love. Athletes are endowed with popularity, fame, and fortune millions only dream of. Because of that fame, the world acknowledges and promotes their stature of greatness to a pinnacle of influence. Whether it's good or bad, either way, they have influence.

Pastors hold sacred credibility with people, but when it is abused, it can lead many to false hope and wounding disappointment.

One of the most influential people of our generation is none other than Tim Tebow. Beginning with the University of Florida Gators, Tim brought unity among people all over the nation with Philippians 4:13 marked on his face during the games. His classic prayer kneel brought great controversy and attention. Yet, amid the media hoopla, he remained humble while directing all the praise to Christ.

One ministry that is important to Tim is the ministry to special needs kids. It's not that Tim is such an awesome influence on his own, but it's the work of Jesus in him.

Watching him acknowledge his love and devotion to Christ on the field and off is nothing less than inspiring. He is one who lives out his faith while using his platform of sports to spread the gospel. He, for one, is a tremendous Godly influence.

Jim Jones, a cult leader, on the other hand, persuaded his followers to participate in a ritual that would take their lives. More than 900 men, women, and children took part in his 1978 dark mass suicide plot in Jonestown, Guyana. How could one man manipulate people to the point they would offer up their families, finances, and freedom in order to obey him? Simply put, influence. Jim offered the people of Jonestown broken and empty promises. He had led them in cult practices. How much influence can one man have? He influenced people not only to believe him, follow him, and buy in to his ideals, but he also influenced them to ultimately carry out this atrocious act, all because of influence.

It's easy to blame political leaders, social poverty, school systems, and other parties for dropping the ball when it comes to Godly influence. But if we really have the guts to look at ourselves, question our intentions, and accept the truth, we will most likely see that it's the lack of Godly influence that can be the reason for our crisis of today. Stop and ask yourself this question, "Have I pointed people to Jesus or me?"

We would all say, "to Jesus, of course." But if you left your position today in leadership, would people pick a side and leave with you or would they stay, realizing God's work must continue and they are a part of that work? OK, don't shoot the messenger here. Self-evaluations can be very uncomfortable but very necessary. We cannot be that

guy who builds his own kingdom in the name of religion. The walls will fall. Have we influenced

Have I pointed people to Jesus or me?

those around us to rise up, to lead with integrity, and never forsake their call?

When we point the attention towards ourselves, we've contaminated our culture. We set as a standard that all we do is within ourselves, thus limiting expansion, limiting growth, and limiting God. Yes, duplicate yourself. Learn to pour into others but allow them the room to grow into what and who God has called them to be. They don't need to be a carbon copy of you but of Christ.

Remember what Paul says in 1 Corinthians 11:1: "Follow my example, as I follow the example of Christ." He was a reflection of Jesus. He was leading the way but not portraying himself to be the way. If you are blessed to have protégés, allow them to learn from your mistakes, take the best you can offer, and then encourage them to expand to what and where God is leading them. We are always better together.

Jesus Christ influenced every person who came in contact with Him. As He walked the Earth, He made eternal differences in the most unlikely people. He influenced leaders, teachers, countrymen, prostitutes, fishermen, and religious leaders. He took advantage of every afforded opportunity when it came to influencing people. His acts of love, His teachings, His kindness, and His captivating words influenced the most casual observers. When it comes to influence, Jesus was and is the most influential person who ever walked the Earth. He was so influential, He compelled a fisherman, a doctor, a tax collector, a zealot, a tradesman, and others of various occupations to abandon their livelihoods in order to follow Him. He chose twelve men to change the world through Him. Jesus sketched the first blueprints of how we not only need to influence others but also pour into them, building a team. This is called discipleship. And based on the principle of discipleship, we are to deepen our lines of influence. People who are desiring to follow Christ will use the influence you have poured into them and pour into others with the same influence. So, the depth at which you influence them will be the starting point for others.

Speaking of deepening your line of influence, football is a sport that can be relatable to just about any age. A football team is layered by first string, second string, and third string. In other words, there is a depth to each team. Or at least there should be. If you want to know the true strength of a team, look at the cross depth of their team. If a star running back was injured in a play, would they have another star just as talented to step in? Would anyone notice? Well, when it comes to the work of a pastor with big dreams and ambitions, you need to duplicate and go deep with your layers. You have to pour into others and equip them to help. Remember, refusal to expand is refusal to grow. As in business, if you plan on moving forward in ministry, you must accommodate growth. You don't wait for growth to happen before you prepare for it. The first signs of growth come due to the preparations you made for that growth. The principle of delegation should be screaming out here! Delegate. Pour into those you can hand off parts of the dream and goals to.

I know, no one really wants to let go! Here are some reasons why you may be apprehensive of delegating:

"I don't think others can do the task quite like me." OK, maybe they can and maybe they can't. That's not the issue. As a father or mother, you have an incredible opportunity to pour into your children. They absorb very quickly. Children of parents who never allow them to experience and learn skills will remain ignorant, not incapable. They will not learn the skill sets you have to offer unless you delegate—allowing them to learn by personal experience. The day will come when you will want them to take care of themselves. Then when they can't, you must realize it's not their fault they have undeveloped skills. They just never had the opportunity to learn. So, delegate. Allow those working with you to try and try again. Allow them to grow.

"I don't like change." Well, if there's any one thing that will remain the same, it's change. Change is inevitable. Change cannot be stopped. It cannot be thwarted. Change will happen with or without you. Change will take place whether you are ready for it or not. Without change, you'll never see a change. Changing your strategy in order to delegate is essential for growth. Embrace change or it will change you.

"I'm too driven to let go." I have only one thing to say about this one. If you are too driven to let go, you will soon find yourself driving down a lonely and limited road.

"They don't understand the dream." If those around you don't understand your dream, it's only because you haven't shared your dream. Leaders must "scream the dream." Let it be heard. When you do, those fans will emerge.

"I'm afraid others will run off ahead of me." No one will be ahead of the visionary. But when they excel, be happy and take it as one of the greatest compliments of your leadership. This means someone has bought into your vision and is now ready to help you take it further than you would have on your own.

"I don't know how." This is an easy one. Give a job or task to someone else. Give others the right and authority to do something you don't have to do. Do only what you can do. Give the rest away.

One of the most incredible accounts in the Bible is actually one of Jesus' greatest miracles, when He fed the five thousand. In Matthew 14:21, He uses the Greek term specifying males when referring to the five thousand. Further He adds, "in addition to women and children," which means there is a high probability there were between fifteen and twenty thousand people in all. But for the sake of the principle of delegation, let's go with fifteen thousand.

First, let's set the stage. Jesus has been teaching and as the day grows older, Jesus realizes the people haven't eaten. Now, they are located in an area where there are no local restaurants, no buffets, and no convenience stores to pop in to grab a quick bite. These are families who are willing to sacrifice a meal in order to hear the life-changing words of Jesus. But that's when Jesus steps in with compassion, realizing their need for food. Jesus tells the disciples to give them something to eat. The challenge and dilemma is that there is no food.

None of the disciples had brought snacks, coolers, or other items for a mega picnic. Simply put, they have nothing. Then one of the disciples comes to Jesus with the news. There is a boy with five barley loaves and two fish. Basically, it is a young boy with his lunch.

To any person, the very thought of bringing a boy's lunch to feed thousands of people would have certainly been ludicrous, impossible, and ridiculous. Can you imagine what the people who were in the close proximity of the conversation would have thought? They may have had the same bewildered demeanor the disciples had when the words, "You feed them," rolled off of Jesus' tongue. "Holy cow!" seems to be an appropriate response right about now.

What a challenge of the mind and heart to conceive and believe. Could it have been at that moment the disciples' hearts were flooded with doubt? Yet, somewhere deep inside them was the seed of faith that afforded the birth of a miracle.

Jesus would not only feed them spiritually, but He would perform one of the most memorable miracles ever—a miracle of meeting the need of a hungry crowd. Put yourself in the shoes of Jesus for a moment. How would you have liked to be the one others turned to in the time of need? How would you have handled the high order of the impossible? How would or could one man facilitate the feeding of that many people?

Jesus takes this meager meal, blesses it, and begins to break it, multiplying every morsel. But how do twelve men feed fifteen thousand or more people a meal? As they began to distribute the fish and bread, there was a miraculous multiplication that took place. One piece of bread now became two, two became four, and four became more. The multiplication of fish was more of a catch than any other disciple had caught. This was a monumental experience.

In order to effectively feed that many people, there had to be delegation. One man blessed the fish, broke the bread, and twelve men served while assimilating among the crowd. There had to be those who assisted them in this amazing feat. The question is how did they do it? Did they seat them by hundreds, fifties, or even smaller units?

The point here is to understand that great accomplishments come through delegating team efforts. With every great victory in life, there lies a structured plan. The structural plan for Jesus was delegating the task of passing out the food to those twelve men, with the help of others who passed along the baskets. Not only did others help with distribution, but they also helped with gathering. Gathering? Yes, gathering. The miracle of feeding all those people was now to be followed by another miracle, which was gathering twelve baskets full of leftovers. How do you have more than you started with? Impossible, unless it is a divine intervention. And I know none of the people, much less the disciples, saw that coming. Twelve men, who probably didn't have a background in waiting tables, would have easily been overwhelmed by the sight of the sea of hungry people. Nonetheless, Jesus handed them the morsels. Yes, Jesus gave these twelve interns in ministry forethought. He affirmed them with a basket of fish and bread which would only be one of hundreds if not thousands. If Jesus had not afforded the opportunity for those men to witness this great work, they would not have learned the act of delegation. Jesus never exercised His right of doing it all Himself. He could have—He's Jesus. But instead, He set the example and displayed how a true leader delegates the dream to fruition. Dreams never come to pass when approached with a selfish heart.

One thing is for sure. If you never allow your dreams and goals to be delegated today, you will remain in the same place tomorrow. Delegation is your catalyst. Delegation is your friend. Learn to embrace delegation. A horrific mistake for anyone to make would be to refuse structured delegations, personally accepting all responsibilities, yet expecting results you would have if you had a team to facilitate your goals. Insanity!

Picture a huge ship on the ocean. You set your coordinates for an island of paradise. However, along the way you encounter a storm. You realize this storm is going to take some navigation skills and hard work from the crew in order to make it through without damaging the ship. As

One thing is for sure. If you never allow your dreams and goals to be delegated today, you will remain in the same place tomorrow.

captain, you call, "All hands on deck!" You give the command for some to hold their stands at board, you give the orders for others to raise the sails, then you order others to secure the cargo. Suddenly, you perceive the crew is not performing their tasks correctly, so you make them all jump ship. That's right, jump ship! "Are you crazy?" you'd ask. You've just sentenced yourself and your crew along with the ship to a brutal and fatal end. Well, not allowing others to help you will have the same effect. You will sabotage your crew and sink your ship! No, no one will do everything perfectly. But neither do any of us. God has set us out to experience some incredible adventures. But if we don't allow the crew to help us, then we too will be operating in insanity—which is the same as attempting to be everywhere, for everything, and for everyone every time!

There are numerous accounts of leaders who have micromanaged their employees in such a way that it drove the creativity, passion, and performance of those employees to a sudden stop. Let me explain. My two sons marched in a high school band. One played French horn and one played snare on the drum line. One afternoon, I noticed their band director's facial expressions were troubled, which led me to believe he was frustrated, so I casually walked over. After some small talk, I asked him if everything was OK. He assured me that he would be fine. We continued to talk for a minute or two and then he said, "I don't get it! Some of these parents are squeezing the life out of these kids when all they need is some room to grow."

He explained, "If you take some water and put it in your hand, you can contain it. But the very moment you squeeze your fist tightly, the water escapes immediately. It will squirt out through your fingers. There's no way to hold onto it. That's what some of these parents are doing to their children."

I must admit, I wasn't expecting that response. However, this was a great illustration explaining how parents should allow kids the room to grow, even though they will make numerous mistakes. It also spoke volumes for those who are in leadership who are squeezing the life out of their teams. If you, as a leader, compress those who are helping facilitate your dream with a tight grip, you can expect their return to be less productive, leaving you to your demise. No one can or wants to live or work in that kind of culture. If you are reading this book and are micromanaging, "driving," or using threats and intimidation tactics to acquire what you want, please stop immediately! It doesn't belong to you. It's God's! So, lead with integrity, honesty, and truth so God's blessings will continue to flow.

When we assume the position of God, we will soon find out we are way over our heads. Lead by example. Model by humility. You must allow those who serve alongside you to grow, create, expand, and flourish amidst their mistakes. Micromanaging will certainly turn opportunity to obligation, while leading will move you from mediocrity to monumental progress.

If God gives you a vision bigger than yourself, awesome! If He gives you a vision bigger than you, then you alone cannot accomplish it. If He gives you this big dream to be accomplished, then don't you think He would want you to bring aboard those who can help accomplish that vision? Whatever He's called you to, He will bring you through. You may have doubts about yourself, but God must believe in you to give you the dream that is passionately burning within you.

Sure, there are questions and concerns, but just know there have been others who have struggled with some of the same issues. Let's take a step back and look at Moses again since he seems to be one who has a lot to offer when it comes to leadership. He was leading approximately three to five million Israelites to the Promised Land. God gave him the vision that the people would be delivered from the Egyptians. Moses' brother, Aaron, was to be his helper, supporter, and verbal communicator since Moses himself had a speech impediment. You see, what God commanded him to do was much bigger than Moses himself. He had to have someone to help him along the way. Why, Jesus himself, called twelve men, His disciples, to carry out the Great Commission. God has never intended for us to be alone except for one time—during prayer.

Speaking of those twelve disciples who followed Jesus, they did learn what true leadership was all about. They walked with Jesus. They talked with Jesus. They

> *Whatever He's called you to, He will bring you through.*

traveled with Jesus. They spent time with Jesus. They ate with Jesus. They followed Jesus. Each day was a day of incredible encounters. And if there is any *one* thing that can be for certain, they failed! And they failed big.

Peter, one of Jesus' closest friends, denied Jesus three times in the same night. He also walked on water until he took his eyes off Jesus and began to sink. On another occasion, Peter cut off a soldier's ear while they were attempting to arrest Jesus. Peter just seems to be "that guy" who always did the wrong thing, at the wrong time, and to the wrong person. He also seemed to open his mouth at the wrong time, speaking the wrong words, to the wrong person. If an event or situation could be sabotaged, he sabotaged it.

But Jesus' leadership and love for Peter was over the top! Jesus allowed Peter to "fail forward." Fail forward? Failing is always perceived in a negative connotation. Why, the word "fail" in itself means to fall short. Instead of condescending or rebuking Peter, Jesus allowed him to fail forward. What Peter didn't realize was that Jesus was allowing him to mess up in order to be propelled to greatness. Peter had to fail in front of a few so he could succeed in reaching many. Looking at not only Peter's life, but all of the disciples, you will see failure at some point and time. There were so many twists and turns, ups and downs of Peter's life that we could have called it a "spiritual roller coaster." Allowing others to fail in order to learn is a vital necessity—a product of delegation. Allowing others to fail forward is one of the greatest signs of compassion and patience in leadership. As a leader, you should be tenderhearted with those you train. You should sympathize with them because you know you were "that guy" who failed once too. You made mistakes. You epicly failed! Don't forget how it felt to disappoint those who were over you. Allow those under you to fail but never allow them to stay there. Take that life-changing moment to teach them how to handle failure.

After Jesus' death, the disciples did what I probably would have done. They went back to doing what they were accustomed to doing. They left the ministry to go back to fishing. In their minds, what else was there? Their best friend, Lord, healer, deliverer, leader, and Savior was gone. Peter, who had denied Christ three times, was now probably wallowing in defeat, discouragement, and disillusionment. They basically went back to where Jesus found them to begin with. They returned to the only thing they knew to do—fish! I'm sure Peter, along with the others, wondered what would happen in the days to come. Could it have been when they were fishing, their minds daydreamed seeing this man named Jesus walk into their world? Could it have been when Peter was fishing that his mind went back to the night he walked on water to meet

Jesus? Could it have been that Peter, amid his epic failure, was hoping once again Jesus could somehow set back time so he might experience once again that life-changing moment when he met Jesus? As Jesus would have it, He did.

Imagine that moment: Peter, with some of the other disciples, is casting nets off the side of the boat. Spending most of their time catching nothing, they turn their boat to shore. As they return to shore, they find Jesus cooking fish for them. Jesus invites those disciples to join him.

As they are eating, Jesus asks Peter a question.
"Peter, do you love Me?"
"Lord, you know that I love you," Peter replies.
Then Jesus says, "Then feed My sheep."

Jesus was affirming Peter. As scripture reveals, Jesus asked Peter three times if he loved Him and commanded Peter to feed His sheep. Three times Peter denied Christ and three times Christ affirmed Peter. Jesus never let Peter go unrestored.

As a leader, what if your fellow minister makes a mistake? How would you react? Would you be the one to help restore, rebuild, and reassure the one you've poured into? Can you allow the mistake to strengthen his character? Could you do it more than once? Now I'm not necessarily speaking of a moral fall—however, it still applies—but the mistakes ministers and leaders alike can make on a daily basis. Can you offer him the same compassionate and comforting acceptance? Can you reinstate the heart that longs to do right? Patience and mercy speak volumes of the leaders who live and apply it. Think about it—without patience and mercy, God would have taken us out a long time ago.

CHAPTER FOUR

What Not to Do

I 've heard many times we learn more of what NOT to do than what TO do. In ministry, I've had the idea that if I only had someplace to go to learn new things, new ideas, new ways, new this, and new that, I could get ahead. Maybe a conference, maybe a rally, or maybe a workshop would make me a better leader. Well, yes all of these can be great tools and strategies. But nothing can take the place of hands-on experience. I guess it would be similar to attempting to carry on a conversation about duck hunting when you've never held a shotgun in your hands. You can't give what you don't know. You can't explain what you've never done. What gives you credibility and allows you to communicate with intelligence is when you've had the opportunity and experience. But once you've participated or actually taken part in a situation, it's then and only then that you become a credible source. And those situations afford learning what NOT to do.

Now, after being in ministry for some time, I've learned that some of the most valuable nuggets have come from learning from other's mistakes. I've watched leaders make great decisions and grave decisions that were quite costly. In a moment, I realized I was thinking to myself, "I'll never do that; that's for sure!" Wisdom is in the listening, watching, and learning from crucial moments. To be the best at something, you really need to know what NOT to do in order to keep from the pitfalls and failures that lie ahead. It's much easier knowing what to do when one is shown what to do, but very few discover what not to do. The idea of learning from others' mistakes is what will keep us from the heartache and disappointments that come from making those mistakes. The greatest asset one can obtain in the midst of encountering a mistake is being able to fail forward into greatness.

The Scripture tells us in 1 Corinthians 10:11, "Now these things happened to them as an example, but they were written down for our instruction, on whom the end of the ages has come."

I want to learn from this Scripture the principle that, "These things were written down for our instruction." If we are able to learn from the past and mistakes made in the past, then we won't fail like those from the past. We must get over ourselves and move forward. And moving forward builds our character and pleases the heart of God.

Speaking of learning what not to do, let me share a story from my younger years. When I was in college I acquired a job working at a winery located just outside the campus in an agricultural zone. It was known as the enology lab. This winery was an asset for many reasons. One reason in particular was to host parties for members of the political and educational realm. Driving onto the property at just the right time of the evening meant you could watch the sun setting behind the vineyards, enhancing the water droplets that glazed the grapes. An early morning drive meant you could see the dew blessing the morning with its presence on the grapes. The manicured landscape was gorgeous. This lab was literally engulfed by a rose garden that contained many varieties of roses. Needless to say, it was a beautiful place of employment.

I began in the cellar of this Swedish-style venue pressing grapes from the vineyard, which happened to be nestled between two rose gardens just outside the back entrance. Every morning there were harvesters who brought crates of grapes into the cellar to be pressed. We actually had an old-style press that we used for demonstrations. It was considered an antique. The floor of the cellar was tiled with two drains that allowed the residue of harvesting to be washed away. On one end of the cellar was a wine storage room, set at a designated temperature for the success of inoculation and storage. Another room on the other end was for champagne that was processed. This cellar, as it was called, was to be pristine at all times. That meant no trash, dirt, grape skins, or any other debris could be on the floor unless it was during harvest time. They trained me as one of the hands who initiated and maintained the inoculation process of the wine. The procedures and hands-on experience taught me a great deal about wine, such as how it was made, stored, and maintained.

My coworker was a young man from Nigeria named Rudolph. He and I worked well together and developed a great friendship. One skill I learned in the lab was how to distinguish rich and flavorful wine from those that were compromised by either high or low acid levels. Yes, there is a difference.

Now, as I said before, the cellar was to be immaculate at all times. In order to keep it clean, one of our jobs was to take large glass containers that had been used in the inoculation process and wash them with soap and scalding water. Then we would prepare them for the next round of inoculation.

One day, Rudolph and I were working diligently in preparation for a special guest to tour the facility. Little did we know the special guest was none other than world-renowned chef Paul Prudhomme. He was an amazing Cajun chef. It was going to be an awesome experience to get to eat some authentic Cajun food and meet Chef Prudhomme. Rudolph and I made sure the storage rooms were prepared for his arrival in the cellar.

As I said before, this cellar was not like most cellars. This cellar was equipped with vats, storage rooms, and wash rooms. The vats held several hundred gallons of juice that had been pressed, mixed, and inoculated. After the grape's juice had been pressed and poured into a vat, sugar, calcium carbonate, and a few more ingredients were stirred and then heated. The mixture was poured into ten-gallon glass containers with an inoculation cap and pressure gauge on top. Then the containers would be placed in a temperature-controlled cellar room where the magic of inoculation would begin. Once the inoculation process was over, the containers were emptied.

This is where the story gets interesting. While washing and moving these containers, I lost grip of one of them, sending it to the tile floor only to shatter into what appeared to be a million pieces. Ok, it *was* a million pieces. Panic set in! For a split second, I could have sworn I lost consciousness from the sheer terror of the idea of my boss finding me standing in the midst of a sea of glass. Just then, the inconceivable happened. The elevator doors opened and, you guessed it, my employer, Dr. Vine, and Chef Prudhomme stepped out. There I stood, just as I had feared moments before, with a look that you'd have when your mom catches you with your hand in the cookie jar. Horrified, I wanted to jump into a cistern and bury my head. Why in the world did this have to happen right now? I was most certain I had just created my own demise. I thought for sure I would hear, "You're fired!"

Ok, stop! Can you feel the awkwardness right about now? I can. But to my surprise and glorious relief, my employer introduced my coworker and me as the hardest working college boys around. He then proceeded to reaffirm me in front of Chef Prudhomme. He patted me on my shoulder as if to say, "It happens to the best of us." He then reached into his pocket, pulled out a twenty-dollar bill, and said, "Why don't you boys go grab some lunch, take a break, then come back and clean up." I never saw that coming!

It was not until a few years later I realized just how great a leader he actually was. And I never knew until a few years later just how valuable that lesson was and would be in the years to come. He taught me two lifelong lessons I am forever grateful for. One was how to treat everyone with respect, whether they are in leadership or service. It didn't matter who was around—a doctor, professor, or Chef Prudhomme—he treated me as an equal, valued employee, and honestly, as a friend. Secondly, he demonstrated how to have self-control in the midst of a difficult time. In other words, he taught me how a true leader acts and reacts in the moment of crisis. As for me, well, he knew I was working hard. He recognized it was an accident. He seized the opportunity to reaffirm me rather than crush me in the presence of a guest. That was great wisdom!

As Scripture tells us in Proverbs 18:21, "The tongue has the power of life and death, and those who love it will eat its fruit." If he had scolded me, embarrassed me, or been condescending towards me, it probably would have taken me quite some time to recover. To say the least, it would have humiliated me beyond repair. Instead, his words were healing while the wound of failure was still fresh.

Proverbs 12:18 states that the tongue of the wise brings healing, and that's exactly what he brought. Needless to say, that day taught me so much about how to handle situations during crisis. But the greatest was obviously what NOT to do. These life lessons can only be taught through experiences. Without these experiences many will tread the thin lines of leadership and dictatorship. Allow me to share a few "what not to do's." It might just save your relationships and ministry.

- Never embarrass others, even when you feel you have the right.
- Never have a knee-jerk response. Get all the information before you react.
- Never use your tongue to even the score.
- Never try accomplishing tasks on your own. You need the help.
- Never isolate yourself. They need you to be a team player.
- Never put yourself in a compromising position.
- Never discredit the talent, validity, and relevance of seasoned ministers.

There have been instances where I've witnessed pastors and leaders handle situations in a less productive manner. I've been in those awkward moments when a leader's decision to correct another person was short of being tactful and respectful. It spoke volumes to me and those around me. I realized just how powerful their words were and how loud their actions spoke. Honestly, my heart felt their shame and guilt as they were shredded up like a piece of paper. Here's a truth: a wise leader never has to verbalize his wisdom. He needs only to demonstrate it through his actions. So, yes, learning what not to do is very important. So, learn from others who are attempting to be everywhere, for everything, and for everyone every time, and then change your course.

CHAPTER FIVE

Be Yourself

Learn to be yourself! It's easy to say and harder to do. We often pattern ourselves after others we admire. There is nothing wrong with that, to a certain degree. You can most definitely learn and glean from others, but when it's time to move forward in your ministry and your life, you need to stretch your wings and fly. So many people never get to taste the freedom that comes from being themselves. Most stay in the nest of security.

Eagles are some of the most majestic birds. Making their homes on the pinnacles of the Earth, they are able to overlook the valleys below for food. These incredible creatures are able to soar at altitudes other birds only dream of flying. They portray the epitome of a warrior. Their shriek of passion can be heard piercing through the skies. Without one simple yet daring step, the eagle would be much like a common chicken, head down, pecking on the ground. That one step is one of character, passion, bravery, and simply life. That one step is leaving the nest for the first time. Why? Well, the nest can be several hundred feet high above jagged rock. Leaving the nest without the faith work of flapping its wings would bring it to a fatal end. One by one, they follow their mother's example by actually taking a leap of faith, a step they believe will usher them into the heavens.

However, there is that one who does not want to follow suit. When the mom sees this eaglet is not participating in this plight for flight, she must take desperate action. She knows if that little warrior doesn't take flight, he will not strengthen his feathers and he will eventually die from lack of food because mom will stop feeding him. So, with nurturing tough love, the mother eagle begins disassembling the nest twig by twig, forcing her little eaglet to face a moment of truth. It is a moment of do-or-die, fall-or-fly. It's at that moment the eaglet must make a life-altering decision. He must fly! We too must take a leap of faith, leaving the nest of security and comfort and fly the heights of wonder to be who God has designed us to be. He's gifted you to be like no one else. If God wanted more of you, He would have made more.

The greatest challenge in anyone's life is to discover who they really are and be the best person they can be. Learning from others is always good, but carbon copies don't have the same value as the original. Take, for instance, the United States Declaration of Independence. Crafted more than 200 years ago, these proposed principles, scored by our founding fathers, have become our nation's creed of passion. You can purchase a copy of the Declaration of Independence on the Internet for about twenty bucks. The

One truth I've discovered is: you'll never fulfill what you are until you know who you are.

papers look like the original, the print looks like the original, the size even looks original. But guess what? It's not the original. It's a copy. Only the original papers have priceless value. You cannot, nor should not, be someone else. Be original! Therein lies your priceless value.

I've always enjoyed talent shows. It's mind blowing to discover how awesome people really are. God has gifted so many of us with so many different skill sets and phenomenal talents. After watching a national TV talent show, I recall hearing one of the judges ask a contestant what or who he wanted to be. His response was quite disappointing to hear. He simply said, "I don't know!" This is not what the judge wanted to hear, nor was the judge's response what the contestant wanted to hear. "You've got to know who you are," the judge said. One truth I've discovered is: you'll never fulfill what you are until you know who you are.

You have to have your own identity. There is so much truth in this statement. You have to know who you are—first in Christ, secondly, in your calling. This is where many people falter because it's an easy fix to be or act like someone else, trying to imitate their passion, strategy, dress, or even mannerisms. God made you to be you! Think about all of the awesome creativity, leadership, teaching, encouragement, and tools others miss out on if you never MOVE INTO YOU! Inside you are those treasures God has placed to be shared the way only you can share them.

So, may I ask you to please, be yourself? Do what only you can do. Stop trying to be everywhere, for everything, and for everyone every time.

CHAPTER SIX

It's Not What You Do,

But How You Do

top the madness! With everything we do, there comes a time when we need to slow down, stop, evaluate, and correct our course! Remember, it's not necessarily what you do to care for others that causes a problem, but maybe it's *how* you are going about it. There are two problems with trying to be a Pop-Up Pastor. First, you will run dead end into yourself, leaving you with burnout and an unhealthy perspective. Second, you will cause others to have a skewed perspective of your sincerity. Your inability to be everywhere, for everything, and for everyone every time will drive you to a faster pace limiting your time with others. It will appear to others you are too busy to bother, or the quality time needed is cut short, leaving others to feel they are unimportant. Listen, our passion for success is the fuel to drive us to the goal. But one thing to remember…the problem in ministry is not the passion but the process. Without a process to channel your passion, you will most definitely find yourself derailed. Passion is a necessity in ministry, and a well-executed process brings peace of mind. We, as pastors, love by default, but our processes must be changed in our settings.

There's only one of you, and if you cap yourself out, there's no more of you to go around. As silly as that may sound, the truth is this: once you get maxed out, there's no more that can be added. At that point, you will be overloaded and on a certain track for burnout. Furthermore, we set examples for others to follow. As leaders, it is important that we be examples that won't create more stress for someone else, but instead examples that will propel others to greatness! Pastors have not only fallen into the spiraling tailspin of attempting to be everywhere, for everything, for everyone every time themselves, but have also set an example for younger ministers to follow. This is often the result of an unrealistic goal their own leaders aimed for and strived for, which leads to an unhealthy expectation from younger pastors or leaders. Either way, it's an unhealthy habit of culture.

There was a quote I saw several years ago you may have heard. It says, "You plan to fail when you fail to plan." I never want to fail! In fact, I don't know of anyone who does, especially in ministry.

You plan to fail when you fail to plan.

The sheer fear of failing keeps many from moving forward into great opportunities. Let me share some lyrics from a song I wrote that conveys how fear keeps us from moving forward: "Some men never brave the sea, for fear it's too wide and deep, only to dream of what might be, but fear of failure has stripped my dream from me."

Failure is a knock-out blow to our ambition. So, because of past failure, many quit trying. Again, no one wants to fail. But when we are placed in a position to be everywhere, for everything, for everyone every time, well, it's inevitable. You will fail! Being sucked into attempting to do this is sometimes from simple tradition. It's expected of pastors by their parishioners, expected of staff by pastors, and everyone else in between, and when one misses one occasion, then it seems to be carved into people's minds that the pastor obviously doesn't care. How far from the truth! And this is one sure way to fail.

One of the most difficult lessons to learn is no matter how much you want to be, you can never be all things to all people all the time and LIVE! You would most certainly drive yourself crazy in the process and be of no value to anyone. Jesus Himself didn't please everyone. Why, some sought to stone Him, some of his closest friends (Mary and Martha) were disappointed in Him because He didn't show up in time to heal their brother from sickness. So, if Jesus didn't please everyone, then what makes us believe that we could? Some people you will never please because they are caught in the cesspool of ritualistic values and practices that expect unrealistic results. In other words, don't allow others to bind you to a practice that is unrealistic. Don't allow the pollution of the Pop-Up Pastor to choke you out of being effective. Work in your skills and wheelhouse and delegate to others what you cannot do.

Mismanagement of ministry and more importantly your time can be detrimental to your sanity and health. In the early years of ministry, it can be easy to accept just about any type of opportunity of ministry. The eagerness and drive of ministry has been known to ambush many, entangling them in a debilitating web of stress. This stress will rob you of the ability to make rational decisions. You could say it takes away your ability to think through. One imperative rule to remember is to never let that happen. Very few take time to evaluate their abilities and capabilities. Rather, they bombard the world of ministry without considering the cost, sacrifices, responsibilities, and the awesome possibilities.

In doing so, you probably will experience firsthand the sheer force and immobilizing presence of the tsunami avalanche of ministry. An avalanche was once described as sounding like an earthquake and an ominous tsunami of snow gliding down the slopes of mountains like a surfer on a wave. Anyone in its way is certain to be rolled over and totally consumed by the white powder monster. There are many who enter ministry with an unbridled desire to do as much as possible for the kingdom. In the process, they begin a very slippery slope in which the business of the opportunity begins to grow, causing a great wave of demand that will only increase. The problem is that those desires are unleashed without thinking through how each opportunity will demand time and commitment. Biting off more than you can chew is hard to swallow. Accepting too many opportunities will leave you worn, burnt out, and wishing you had never taken that bite of responsibility.

Juggling is a skill and art that intrigues audiences of all ages. Clowns, circus acts, and entertainers alike juggle just about anything they can get their hands on. One of my friends is an excellent juggler and entertainer in Florida. Watching him is quite impressive as he juggles bowling pins, knives, balls, handkerchiefs, and just about anything.

It's quite humorous to watch as he begins to juggle with three pins, then adds another and another and yet another. It all seems so easy until there is *the* one that will be one too many. That one will send all of the juggling pieces crashing down to the ground. Needless to say, jugglers are incredible artists and managers of components. Ministry juggling is an art and skill as well. Why? Because ministry is multifaceted. Without focus and prioritization of your gifts and calling, it becomes easy to take on more than you can handle. Furthermore, attempting to juggle them all will either suppress productivity or cause a resentful collapse of it all. Manage your time and opportunities well or you will find yourself dropping the pins of ministry in frustration. Too many irons in the fire will get you burned. Focus on what gives you the most joy and attack!

If the demand of ministry is engulfing your time away from your own family, then you are chained to the ministry beast. It will drag you through the mud. I'm not saying ministry is bad, but it's the demand of ministry without help that completely exhausts you. If you are able in your season of life to manage multiple ministries without jeopardizing some time with your family, then do it with great joy, yet cautiously. If you are in a season of life with family and you are trying to be everywhere, for everything, and for everyone every time, and this is speaking to you, may I encourage you to stop and evaluate what and who you are doing it for? Then take the steps to balance and prioritize your life. If you do, you will find incredible release and freedom. And your family will thank you.

CHAPTER SEVEN

Stick to Your Guns

L eading isn't always easy, but it sure is rewarding. As pastors and leaders, we shepherd flocks of people. We look over the well-being of those whom Father God has entrusted to us. Realizing the responsibility God has placed on us as leaders should encourage us to lead with humility, yet with authority.

Leadership can often be a lonely place. How, you ask? When everyone else seems to be taking shortcuts in performance, stooping below the maturity limbo bar or taking the self-centered road, you as a leader must remain focused and firm in what you believe. When others ask you to join in with their lackadaisical actions, you refrain. True leaders may not be at the top of the popularity pole, but they must be at the top of the integrity pole because leaders are expected to go the extra mile in all you do— and rightfully so. As leaders, you lead. You set examples. You set the tone for meetings. You give vision. You give direction. And you give all you have, mind, heart, soul, and strength to the dreams God's placed in your heart. It takes a lot of stamina, strength, and pure grit to stick to your guns. You simply stick to what you believe is true! In other words, you'll be the last one to turn out the lights!

In all seriousness, as a leader you have to stick to your guns in what you believe, especially when you are the only one who believes it. According to the dictionary, the phrase "sticking to your guns" actually means to "refuse to compromise or change, despite criticism." In an article posted by the Matador Network called *10 Revolutionary Acts of Courage by Ordinary People*, Dr. Martin Luther King was named one of the greatest leaders of the 20th century!

The article stated, "One of the finest orators and civil rights leaders of the 20th century, Martin Luther King Jr. did much to change the United States' policy on racial discrimination."

After helping to launch the Civil Rights Movement by heading the 1955 Montgomery Bus Boycott, King founded the Southern Christian Leadership Conference, a black religious organization that directed nonviolent protests against segregationist authorities throughout the 1960s.

The zenith of Dr. King's career came on August 28, 1963, with his "I Have a Dream" speech, given at the March on Washington for Jobs and Freedom.

On the symbolic steps of the Lincoln Memorial, King spoke to two- to three-hundred-thousand dissidents and millions of television viewers, rallying for a world free of prejudice in which people would not be "judged by the color of their skin, but by the content of their character."

Dr. King's historic speech was a major deciding factor in the passage of the National Voting Act and Civil Rights Act.

For his part in advocating racial harmony and equality through nonviolent means, King became the youngest ever recipient of the Nobel Peace Prize in 1964. He is only one of many leaders who sacrificed not only their time but also their lives in standing for what they believed.

When taking a step of faith in unforeseen territory, stick to your guns. When criticized for doing the right thing, stick to your guns. When you believe in your heart your dreams must come true, stick to your guns. Even though you may face criticism, you must remain firm. When you believe in something and take a stand, you can always count on opposition. At that moment, you not only have to know what you believe, but you must believe what you believe! You must have deep roots in what you believe because the winds of disagreement and disapproval will beat down against the very foundation of your faith. And as the old saying goes, "If you don't stand for something, you'll fall for anything." Well, it's true. It's vital for you as a leader to display a strong sense of boldness while wearing the resolute armor that renders you immovable and unshakable in what you stand for.

Wrestling against being everywhere, for everything, and for everyone every time is exhausting. You most certainly will be challenged by the world's culture. Some of the opposition may

If you don't stand for something, you'll fall for anything.

be from the very ones who lead YOU. Being everywhere, for everything, and for everyone every time may be expected of you by those you serve alongside. Leaders over you may be the very ones living out the Pop-Up Pastor life, but that doesn't mean you should.

Two young brothers were jumping off the side of a cliff from some rocks into a river. The parents turned up just in time to watch their children jump. The mother screamed, "Hey, have you lost your mind! Don't you know you could have been killed?"

As the boys emerged from the river, the parents asked them, "Why did you jump off those rocks?" The younger boy answered, "Everyone else was doing it." Their mother with a very sarcastic and condescending tone asked, "And if everyone else told you to jump off a cliff, would you do that too?" The little boy, displaying a mischievous grin said, "Mom, we pretty much did." You see, if you follow someone's actions just because of their example, you may be in for some rough roads. Ask the Holy Spirit to guide you and give you insight for your decisions and direction, and He most certainly will.

If you currently operate or have been operating under the laws of the Pop-Up Pastor, may I talk you in off the ledge for a moment before you plunge to your certain burnout? You must stick to your guns when life throws its weight onto your plate. Don't accept more than what you can handle, especially when attempting to be everywhere, for everyone, every time. According to Church Leadership's website http://www.churchleadership.org, there are many pastors and leaders who struggle with depression, fatigue, stress, and burnout. In the *Statistics of Pastors: 2016*, it is reported that:

- 54 percent of pastors work more than 55 hours a week
- 54 percent are overworked
- 43 percent are overstressed

- 35 percent battle depression
- 26 percent are overly fatigued
- 28 percent are spiritually undernourished
- 23 percent are still distant to their families
- 18 percent work more than 70 hours a week and face unreasonable challenges
- 9 percent are burned out
- Yet, 90 percent feel honored to be a pastor!

Most every pastor recognizes the awesome yet sobering position of his or her calling. While ministry is very emotionally and mentally taxing, it is the most rewarding of opportunities. Pastors and leaders alike are drawn to the raw and passionate calling of ministry, which is loving and reaching people, for the hearts of pastors beat with relentless passion for reaching God's most precious creation—people!

By surveying the statistics, it becomes very evident that the personal problems pastors face today aren't necessarily related to their calling. Instead, it's the facilitation of their calling in ministry. It's not "what we do" in ministry but it's "how we do it" in ministry. Stress, fatigue, and depression can most certainly be the culprits of troubled ministers. And these culprits can most certainly be the tell-all signs of a minister who is attempting to be everywhere, for everything, and for everyone every time.

If the above statistics are accurate, then we must acknowledge that over half of all leaders and pastors are facing a defiant culture. This culture, which is so unhealthy, has to change if we are to become more efficient and successful in ministry. Statistics show that we, as leaders and pastors, are driven by passion, but our strategies and facilitating systems fall short, unfortunately at the cost of our own families. That's why you must buckle up, stand firm in your belief that you cannot and should not be everywhere, for everything, and for everyone every time.

It was a beautiful Saturday morning and my dad had just given me a crisp dollar bill for my weekly allowance. I loved getting that dollar from my dad. On this particular Saturday, a local convenience store was advertising a sale for one of my favorite candy bars, the Marathon Bar. It was eight inches of braided caramel covered in milk chocolate. One and one-half inches thick of pure joy. It was awesome! As a kid, it was the ultimate of goodness.

The store was approximately one hundred yards from my house. So, I frequented that store every Saturday in hopes of purchasing a toy or in this case, the Marathon Bar. As I walked through the doors, I noticed a sign that read, "Marathon Bars 10 cents." What?! You've got to be kidding! Then I did what any mature seven-year-old would do when faced with this kind of dilemma. I bought ten! With a few extra cents for taxes I purchased ten Marathon Bars with the full intention of eating every last one of them before I walked back home. Tearing off the wrapper of the first bar, I crammed my mouth full of that sweet flavor of chocolate and caramel. I consumed the first bar much like a vacuum cleaner. The second bar was much like the first but with a bit more enthusiasm since the first went down so quickly. My candy indulgence had reached euphoria until about the seventh bar. At this point, my eating frenzy was like a bed of piranhas attacking a slab of protein.

But then, all of a sudden—and may I reiterate, all of a sudden—my world turned upside down along with my stomach. It felt as if I had ingested a vile substance that must be purged immediately. And that's exactly what happened. I'm most certain I threw up anything I had ever eaten since I was born! It was one of the worst experiences ever at that age. Picture the Poás Volcano, the most volatile volcano in Costa Rica and most likely the world, spewing out it's fury into the atmosphere... Now you get the picture? I was sick! Needless to say, I never finished bar eight, nine, or ten. I'm pretty certain that I didn't eat another Marathon Bar for quite some time.

There are two points here worthy of notice. One is, if you bite off more than you can chew, you will suffer the consequences. If you want something so bad you'll do anything to get it, you too will get all that it brings. Eating all that chocolate and caramel at once brought the revenge of the invasion of the sugar rush. The desire to do great things is admirable but trying to swallow all of it yourself will make you ill. Having too much of anything is not wise. Saying yes to everything isn't the wisest decision either. You must stick to your guns when those extra demands come along.

Secondly, apply your "no!" Saying no isn't always a negative response. Sometimes saying no is the smartest thing you could do. Lysa Terkeurst's book titled *Your Best Yes* gives a great principle when using "yes"

> *Sometimes saying no is the smartest thing you could do.*

and "no" as an answer that will occupy your time. She states that when you give an answer of yes, stop and ask, is it your best yes? In other words, when you say yes, is it the best use of your time? Because when you say yes to one thing, you are saying no to another. Sticking to your guns when you make a decision is crucial no matter the opposition that may come.

Once you determine to not attempt to be everywhere, for everything, and for everyone every time, just make sure you remain firm in your decision—not saying yes again, succumbing to its chains of imprisonment. So, if you are a pastor or leader who is serving under a current culture of a passionate faux pas, then please put on the brakes and assess your life and ministry.

Psalm 46:10 gives us a command when it says, "Be still, and know that I AM God; I will be exalted among the nations, I will be exalted in the earth." At the beginning of that Scripture, the sentence uses a comma denoting a single thought which is, be still! For many, being still is a lost art. Even those of you who have a desire to be still regularly fight the hypnotic cultural tugs of dinners, movies, sports, picnics, parks, concerts, and school functions. Taking time to pray and seek God has always been and always will be the key in understanding His will and direction for our lives. If we rush toward anything, may it be rushing into His presence. When you do take time to seek God, He will most definitely help you prioritize your life.

CHAPTER EIGHT

Settle Down and Breathe

They aren't your enemy. I'm referring to pastors and/or leaders who may be placing more responsibilities on you than you are able to accomplish. I'm referring to those believers who aren't necessarily acting as Christians. Occasions occur when we feel others are being less than fair. When that happens, many pull the "enemy" card. They pray asking God to stop the hand of those who mistreat them, misuse them, and certainly take advantage of them.

This becomes especially complicated when it is your superiors or spiritual fathers. One of the most difficult things to do is confront your superiors when an issue arises worthy of attention. Your relationship with your employer should be open and transparent without fear of being blasted or talked about when you leave. Trust is huge! But regardless of the relationship, you cannot fold when you know what is right. So, if you find yourself struggling to be everywhere, for everything, and for everyone every time then you may need to speak to your employer, leader, and/or pastor about your situation.

Don't stop reading and don't throw this book across the room. Let this set in. I know it seems like I can hear you saying to yourself right now, "I would never be able to do that. I would be fired," or "I don't want to rock the boat." Please hear these words: people have more respect for those who stand with passion and stick to their guns for what they believe in than those who cower down at the first sign of opposition. The old adage applies here: "Wishy-washy thinking will start your boat to sinking."

Not standing up for what you believe in will paralyze your ability to walk in confidence. Leaders who lead, or should I say manipulate, staff by intimidation are struggling themselves for validation and suffer from lack of self-confidence. This kind of leader is the one you'll never grow from but can certainly learn "what NOT to do" from.

A leader who's not willing to hear your heart and concern isn't necessarily concerned about your personal growth or your relationship.

Now, if and when that time comes to speak to your pastor or leader, please be careful and never commit the Three Ds of Disaster!

The first "D" is disrespect. Never allow the perception that you have the right to put your leader in his place take root in your mind. We are commanded in God's word to submit to our employer's authority, direction, and leadership. The moment you feel you have that right, then it's time to be released. When you respect them and their office, they will respect you.

The next "D" stands for demean. Never bring dishonor or attempt to strip them of their dignity. Treat them with the utmost honor, for they are God's man or woman of office whether they are acting it or not. You remain intact.

The third "D" stands for demand. Never demand action. Demanding closes the door for negotiations with anyone. You, as an employee, don't have the right. Let me explain. You as a believer in Christ are to exemplify holiness, purity, self-control, and most importantly, love, even if you are the only one practicing them. Never allow circumstances to rob you of your character. My grandmother used to say, "I'd rather be treated wrongly than treating someone else wrongly." There's a lot of truth here with a ton of Godly wisdom. Allow God to work it out for you. Your pastor, you, and anyone else who's a believer are siblings in one family—the family of God. So, your leader is NOT your enemy, even though the line can

Never allow circumstances to rob you of your character.

be blurred by some actions. Be careful not to cross that line when it comes to asking God to fight your battle when it is between two believers. Instead, pray for wisdom and favor as you approach the moment of conversation. There is no appropriate battle between family members. Father knows how to handle His children. When siblings argue, fuss, and fight, then Father steps in to straighten it out. It's much like when all dads have said to their children in the car, "Don't make me come back there!" My advice? Don't be the kid starting the fight!

One of the most prodigious stories relating the principles of rights as a believer can be found in an obscure and most likely uninhabited cave where David and his men hid while escaping Saul's jealous pursuit.

After Saul returned from pursuing the Philistines, he was told, "David is in the desert of En Gedi." So Saul took three thousand able young men from all Israel and set out to look for David and his men near the crags of the wild goats.

He came to the sheep pens along the way; a cave was there, and Saul went in to relieve himself. David and his men were far back in the cave. The men said, "This is the day the Lord spoke of when he said to you, 'I will give your enemy into your hands for you to deal with as you wish.'" Then David crept up unnoticed and cut off a corner of Saul's robe.

Afterward, David was conscience-stricken for having cut off a corner of his robe. He said to his men, "The Lord forbid that I should do such a thing to my master, the Lord's anointed, or lay my hand on him; for he is the anointed of the Lord." With these words David sharply rebuked his men and did not allow them to attack Saul. And Saul left the cave and went his way. (*1 Samuel 24:1-7*)

Even though some of David's men encouraged him to seize the opportunity to eradicate Saul's deranged state of kingship, he would not allow himself to be drawn into the trap of rights. Do you believe David had the right to kill Saul? Do you believe David should have taken the opportunity to end the reign of Saul? I believe most of us would agree with David's men, especially knowing Saul had tried to pin David to the wall with his spear. Saul was obviously jealous of David. David's favor and promissory kingship of Israel was tormenting to Saul. Instead of Saul embracing the friendship of David, he determined to annihilate him, securing and prolonging his throne as king. However, David did not exercise his right, nor did he listen to his men who tried to convince him to take advantage of the opportunity to take Saul's life. Instead he chose to exercise his right of respect. He chose the path of a true king. David had the wisdom to choose the higher road of leadership by recognizing the anointing God placed on Saul's life. If Saul's reign was to end, it would end by divine design. All David needed to do was to sit back and let God deal with Saul. David would not bring the Three Ds of Disaster upon Saul. Once again, David exemplified a man after God's own heart—a heart of mercy, grace, and forbearance.

If you discover yourself facing the hardships of a leader's madness, allow God to deal with them. Show mercy, grace, and forbearance, realizing they are over you in the Lord. You may not understand their actions, you may not agree with their methods, but you must honor the position.

Don't be afraid or intimidated by those that rule with an iron fist. Stand up for yourself! No, I never said be disrespectful or rude. Nor would I ever suggest such an inappropriate reaction. I would simply encourage you to respectfully and humbly express your concerns and needs to the pastor or leader. Just make sure your concerns and needs are viable. I would also encourage you to communicate the need for assistance when you do recognize your limits. It is possible for a pastor's or leader's passion to unintentionally drive his or her employees to unrealistic expectations and goals. You must render the realistic. Someone who has an unhealthy work ethic can drive another with unhealthy goals. It becomes "the more you do, the more is expected of you." It is then that you must stand for yourself, communicating your concerns with integrity and gallant poise. For it is in this moment that you will gain respect.

Validation is the fuel igniting the passion to drive your vision to a whole new level. But when validation is absent, the vision is pushed and pulled by mere hopelessness. This type of attitude can be seen in those who have made their beds of victimization. Let me explain. Some leaders and pastors have expounded on just how incredible their burdens were. Yes, they have tremendous burdens. But let's clarify. These are burdens of a heart for the people they lead and not necessarily burdens of to-dos. They are not the kind of burdens where legitimacy abounds, but instead with the martyr's mentality. This mentality is baked in "woe is me." Did I just get tickets to "Gloat-Fest" or the "Woe Is Me" tour?

Honestly, no one wants or cares about hearing that. Yet you notice somewhat of a pitiful "woe is me" expression on their faces while a boatload of their "troubles" roll out like a kid's Christmas list. It's as if they gloat in their own weight of misery.

At first glance, it appears as, "the more misery, the better I feel." So, why do people do it? Is it for the love of agony, is it bragging rights of business, or does it provide a feeling of credibility when being stretched beyond human limits—or at least their ability? Maybe you are thinking, "Hey, now that sounds just like (insert name here)." Or better yet, could it possibly be you? This is that moment I would ask you not to shoot the messenger. If you are looking into the mirror of truth right about now, then I know this isn't very pleasant. But stop and take a look.

Have you ever gotten dressed and thought to yourself, "I'm looking good!" But then you take a look in the mirror of reality and the truth kicks in. At that moment you ask, "Have I lost my mind?" It sounds funny until it's you who is looking in the mirror. The mirror of reality can be quite revealing and humbling at the same time. I've stared into that intimidating mirror many times, wondering if my life was out of balance. The answer to that question was yes.

The reason for being out of balance was due to one very important truth: validation. I needed validation.

To be very transparent, there were times I felt if I wasn't busy, then I wasn't needed or important. Wow! How could I have thought such things? Validation doesn't come from busyness. Validation doesn't come from others, no matter what they perceive of you. God alone validates us. He validates our calling. He validates our ministry, not busyness. Just because someone is busy doesn't necessarily mean they are needed. Maybe we are too busy because we desire to be validated by others. And for that reason, we agree to be everywhere, for everything, and for everyone every time. Don't be fooled. Being busier doesn't mean you are accomplishing great things. It could be that you are attempting great things, just in the wrong way. I believed that being busier was better. Busier isn't always better. Nothing is wrong with being busy, as long as busy is in balance.

When I began in ministry my goal was to be as busy as possible. I believed the more calls for ministry I received, the more successful I would be. Was I busier? Yes. Successful? Maybe?

But there's more to the story. It was a time when God had blessed me with a beautiful wife who gave me two boys who captured my heart. It was also a time when ministry opportunities were readily available. Amidst the blessings, I knew there was healthy balance. There were days I wrestled with the call of being everywhere, for everything, and for everyone every time. And there were days I struggled to be home with my family. Needless to say, it was a different season in life. The boys needed me. They needed consistency, they needed regimen, and they needed their dad. Many nights were spent away in cities where ministry called. Many opportunities allowed my family to accompany me and it was great! However, road life wasn't necessarily a place to raise a family. I would never say anyone whose family is on the road is neglecting their family. I'm just saying the road life is hard on anyone, especially an entire family.

Another important note here worthy of mention. Just because you DO get asked to go and minister, it doesn't mean you should. Not every opportunity is one you should take. You should stop, pray, and consider your time, your availability, and the value. Ministry opportunities are always readily available. If you are waiting on someone to call you for ministry, then you should revisit ministry all together. The only limitations of ministry are the limitations you put on yourself. Be careful not to get caught up in the professional ministry loop which deems you are successful only if you are busy. Many believe if you are in "the loop" of ministry, you will be successful. Wrong! It's the daily availability to be used by God no matter where you are that makes you successful. It's Jesus who calls us successful, not another appointment. Just be available!

Now personally, I love staying busy. I excel in get-it-done mode. However, I try and strategize how the dreams and goals can be accomplished with others' help. One important truth to remember here is that we are always better together. Victories are not won by superstars as one might think. Victories are won by team effort. If you are able to accomplish your dream by yourself, well, that dream isn't big enough.

Being busier doesn't mean you are accomplishing great things.

One of sports' greatest assets is building teams, and teams are about wins. Wins come by team efforts, whether you are in a corporation, small business, or church. Now, there are a couple of truths about building teams that always need to be in the back of your mind. First, teams aren't built overnight. Time is the incubator for team building. Over time, you develop relationships which become the glue of your organization.

The second truth about team building is the truth about trust. Trust is the building block for team building. Whether it is military, entertainment, construction, or sports, all dreams are reached through teamwork, but your team will not survive without trust. If you decide to accomplish your dreams by yourself, you are telling others you don't trust them. At that point, you are limiting yourself for growth and expansion. When you lose trust in someone, you might as well be pulling the plug out of your boat. A lack of trust in others can conform you into a lone ranger. When you stop to think about it, anytime you want to do things by yourself, it's like a child holding all of their toys, not willing to let others play. It won't take long to realize that you are by yourself. We all want to win and winning comes through teamwork.

Football is a great example. Football games are not won by one person. Sure, you have a running back or quarterback who gets most of the attention. But don't forget the linemen who are literally taking the hits to protect, creating opportunities to score. It's all team effort. That's why it can be compared to ministry leadership. You have a lead pastor who must throw the ball of delegation to one of the optional receivers in order to get the touchdown. It's never a one-man show. You may have a quarterback who decides to run with the ball, but these are few and far between. A pastor or leader may be able to have a score in ministry a few times, but it is the exception. It takes the team. So, attempting to accomplish goals and dreams by yourself is a recipe for disaster, and to be everywhere, for everything, and for everyone every time will only get you sacked when you're least expecting it.

Another culprit of ministry calamity is comparison. Comparison, when injected in the culture, is a deadly poison that runs slowly through the life blood of any leadership. Anytime you compare yourself to another's works, abilities, or ministry, you are subjecting yourself to an arduous and painful death. Comparison will also put a ceiling on your performance. Why? The reason is that you will only strive to be a little bit better than the one you are comparing yourself to. Comparison goes a lot deeper than the level at which you compare yourself or works too. You should be reaching the goals and dreams of your own—

> *Comparison, when injected in the culture, is a deadly poison that runs slowly through the life blood of any leadership.*

the dreams God has given you. Instead of hearing from God, who has your dreams, goals, and passions in your favor, you decide to emulate a totally different set of dreams, goals, and passions that have never been, nor will ever be, your own. It's difficult for many to understand you cannot be someone else because their mindset is not set on being an original. It is set on what they deem as admirable.

Of course, you will be influenced by others. There's no way around it. We all learn and absorb from others about the dos and don'ts of pastoring and leadership. We absorb some good, some bad, and some uncertainties from people whom we either work for or work with. There are great leaders and there are those who are challenged to be great. The main point here is to understand you must be you! Being influenced by the right source is a great idea, but you still need to proceed with caution. The world doesn't need carbon copies of others, but originals. It's great to be mentored. It's great to glean from others. Take all of it in and allow yourself to be yourself. If you are a carbon copy of someone else, you will never accomplish what God has for you. You shouldn't live out someone else's dreams. Live your own. Only you can be what He's designed you to be and accomplish what He's given you to accomplish.

The struggles are real but not realistic. Pastors, teachers, artists, and leaders can get construed on how tos when comparing their results with others. You can't, nor should you. Yes, we can all agree once again that gleaning from others is profitable. Being mentored is invaluable. But comparison is just unwise and foolish. If you are mimicking another's behavior, procedure, or style, just make sure you leave room for originality. Otherwise, you may come off as a bad Elvis impersonator, thank you very much!

Comparing your life, time, skills, and opportunities with others will leave you with a feeling of inadequacy one-hundred percent of the time. Before you match up your life to others, take a moment and evaluate the season of life you are in. Not everyone's seasons are equal. Your season isn't going to be the same as others' seasons in life. The dynamics are different, life variables are different, and their goals are different. Never compare your behind-the-scenes life to others' on-stage life. If you do, you will be comparing your worst moment against their best. It's unfair, it's unacceptable, and it's absurd.

So, let's look at one of the leading epic problems of young leaders. The problem is not their leadership, but the problem is leadership they have been given to follow. Leaders, this is not our game or claim to fame. Our responsibility as leaders is creating a healthy learning experience for those who follow us. If we lead the younger generation to believe they should be meeting our status quo as seasoned ministry veterans, then we've done an injustice. I've known those who have emulated their mentors but with fewer results, which brought discouragement and disillusionment. The last thing any new minister needs is discouragement.

As a kid whose grandfather owned a dairy farm, I watched as cattle were given tags that were attached to their ears, noting they belonged to my grandfather. This tag was a modern-day branding. These tags adorned each animal with a number to identify who they belonged to in case they happened to escape the farm's pastures.

No matter where they went, they could not escape their brand. As I think about those ministers who embrace the calling on their lives, I can't help but hurt and grieve over the ones who have been branded or tagged as a failure. No matter where they go, the tag or brand identifies them. The most heart breaking of all is not all of their failures were embraced as learning experiences. Not all of their mistakes were forgiven, just branded. To be honest, not all of their mistakes were their fault. Some of those mistakes were made because someone along the way taught them how to do something the wrong way.

Think about this. What if one generation taught the next generation who taught the next generation the way to worship God was to build a statue of an angel and bow down to it? Each generation would be wrong. By default, all generations would make the same mistake because they were falsely educated. If one teaches another that ministry is being everywhere, for everything, and for everyone every time, then by default, the next minister follows suit. But he would also be wrong. He would be branded by his mistakes. Until the cycle is broken, the cyclical effect continues. Leaders should step up, lead the ones who God has entrusted to them, and break the cycle of senseless pressure and obligations they can't keep. If only leaders could intentionally mentor those entrusted to them and give them permission to fail forward. They need to know if they do make a mistake, it's not sudden death, but a time to learn and move forward. The first time a child attempts to ride a bike and falls, the father doesn't sell the bike and tell him to just quit. No. Love, mercy, and grace emerges as he picks up the child, wipes the tears from his eyes and some dirt from his knees, puts him back on the bike, and then empowers him to try again. Rest assured, mistakes without grace are failures branded in the heart and mind.

Let's make this a bit more personal. If you are a young minister or leader, you are probably hungry and eager for pure and raw ministry. Your heart is full of zeal and fire to reach a world of hurting people. You long to run for the lead. Yet, you will need the instruction and a father's heart in ministry to nurture you through the duration of mentorship. Now for those who are seasoned leaders and ministers, you need to embrace the call, obligation, and opportunity of mentorship. If you as a leader aren't open and eager to teach and bless the younger ministers, equipping them for ministry and taking the time to pour yourself into them, then shame on you as their mentor! Please don't miss one of the greatest moments in life, which is affirming and crediting those younger ministers into a position of leadership. They are depending on you for direction, wisdom, and encouragement.

Paul wrote to Timothy encouraging him to lead by example and not allow others to look down on him because of his young age. Timothy, a young man of power and grace, obviously marked with the Spirit of the Lord, seemed to be confronted by the older men of faith who struggled with his position. Paul encouraged him to live a life before the leaders in such a way that they would be reminded of the raw and affectionate passion in which they themselves had been challenged to live. Here are some absolutes worthy of mention.

The driving force in our lives is the Spirit of God, who lives in us. We in ourselves will not and cannot love others the way He desires us to, unless it comes from Him. The drive and passion we have to win and love others is God Himself flowing through us. The drive is Him, the passion is Him. For He is love! His desire to bless us is deeper than ours. His longing for others to know Him is deeper than ours. His love to change the world goes to a much greater depth than we could ever imagine.

We are to exemplify the fullness of our faith with wisdom, leading those around us with a servant's heart. Serving others will always be at the crux of our faith. Jesus came to be a servant, not to be served. Philippians

2 reveals the purpose and passion of Jesus. He came as a servant, even unto death on a cross.

It's not our responsibility to save others; it's our responsibility to be a servant to others. In the past, along with trying to be everywhere, for everything, and for everyone every time, I began placing too much pressure and stress on myself. Let me explain. In the early years of ministry, I was traveling, singing and sharing the gospel. One night, as I approached the end of the night, I gave the audience an opportunity to make a decision to follow Christ. Nights before, there had been many who came to make that decision. However, this night was totally the opposite. Once the night, was over I began to question every word and song, examining, whether or not I should have done or said what I did. Alert! Alert! There was a lot of "I" in that statement. The very fact that "I" did anything is the very core of the problem. Just as soon as those thoughts came to mind, the Lord spoke a very profound statement into my heart. He reminded me that "I" am not the Savior; He is. He didn't call me to be a savior. He called me to be the servant. At that moment, all the stress and worry left as quickly as it came to mind. Finally, the freedom from self-inflicted pressure had dissipated. It is all up to the Holy Spirit to draw people unto Himself and it is all up to Him to save them. As a minister, it is our privilege to be a part of His work by using us and our gifts to pave the way. It is our honor to observe the work of our Heavenly Father.

We, as leaders, are to set the example worthy of following and patterning after. If you were to evaluate your life, deeds, and actions, would they merit the honor and phrase the apostle Paul claimed when he said, "Follow me as I follow Christ"? Wow! He was so certain and confident of his faith and life that he was willing to challenge others to just do what he does. Could you challenge others to follow you as you follow Christ? In other words, I believe it is safe to restate it this way: "Just do what I do and you'll do great!" Many might shudder at the thought, but why are we not living what we believe? Are we not confident in how we live, act, and do life? If not, change it!

If we learn to delegate in order to grow, then we assuredly will embrace the flood of blessings God has in store for those who belong to him. The very principle of delegating is aligning the ministry for growth. Refusing to delegate would be comparable to taking a water hose, turning on the water, and then crimping the flow. It will back up. It will not flow as designed. It will actually build up back pressure, weakening the lining of the hose until the hose explodes. If you try doing everything yourself, you will experience the same outcome. Release the crimp and let ministry flow. You will then experience the growth and joy of ministry.

Living in balance in faith and realizing it's about Jesus and not us will keep us aligned with His will and purpose. It is easy for most people to experience some growth, and while doing so, take on too much of the idea of "it is what I did" ideology. Not that any of us would intentionally think this, but it is in the heart that one can take on ownership of Father's work. I would not take a gift from a friend and call it my own. We are the gifts to be used by Father and not the other way around.

As we strive for excellence in leadership, let us not fall into the black hole of attempting to be everywhere, for everything, and for everyone every time. For some, it will take some practice. For some it will take time. For some it will take dedication and commitment to NOT become a Pop-Up Pastor. It will take guts to say no when you feel pressured to say yes. It will take consistency to become what you desire to be. It will take practice. But don't worry! You can do it! The Holy Spirit will help you as you open yourself to Him, giving Him permission to radically change your thinking. When you do, think about how much more freedom you will have doing what you love to do. Think about less stress of doing it all yourself. Just imagine the growth that will come by allowing others to help you bring about the vision Father has placed in you.

ACKNOWLEDGEMENTS

First and foremost, I would like to thank Jesus for His unfailing love, overwhelming compassion, and relentless pursuit of someone like me. I would also like to thank Him for allowing me this opportunity to share my heart with others.

Thank you to my friend, Tanya Bumgardner, for her guidance, editing, and organization in this project. She deserves a gold medal for putting up with my amateur tendencies.

I would also like to thank Buddy Smith of American Family Association (AFA) and American Family Radio (AFR) for his friendship and leadership. He has honored me with words of affirmation during this project.

Thank you to Randall Murphree, also of AFA, for his friendship, encouragement, and editing. He is amazing!

These acknowledgements would not be complete without the mention of some incredible pastors and leaders who may not realize just how much they have impacted my life. Thank you to Buddy Smith, Joel Smith, Steve McCullar, Doug Anderson, and Gary Sears. I am blessed and honored to call them my friends!

If you are reading this book, then please accept my utmost thanks for giving your valuable time to share these pages, hear my heart, and allow Jesus to speak into your heart.

The Lord bless you and keep you;
The Lord make His face shine upon you,
And be gracious to you;
And give you peace.
Numbers 6:24-26

ABOUT THE AUTHOR

Kevin McHann is a children's pastor who loves the world of ministry, theater, and productions. He's married to Angie and is blessed with two sons, Mason and Jordan, along with a daughter-in-love, Mallory. He loves to write cinematic scores, discipleship curriculum, kids' devotions, and musical productions. His first love was playing drums of any size and type. Kevin's repertoire also includes designing production sets and props, working out, and recently, as you now know, adventuring into writing a book. He can be found randomly hunting hogs or riding his mountain bike.

He traveled the country for more than twelve years as the keynote speaker at KIDFEST, a weekend of amazing fun and ministry for elementary-age children. He also conducted kids' crusades for years before accepting his first church staff position as children's pastor. One of his favorite quotes he lives by is, "Creativity is intelligence having fun."

www.ingramcontent.com/pod-product-compliance
Lightning Source LLC
LaVergne TN
LVHW011208080426
835508LV00007B/678